The Realist's Guide to Redistricting

Avoiding the Legal Pitfalls

SECOND EDITION

J. Gerald Hebert, Paul M. Smith,
Martina E. Vandenberg and Michael B. DeSanctis

Defending Liberty
Pursuing Justice

Section of Administrative Law and Regulatory Practice

Cover design by ABA Publishing

14 13 12 11 10   5 4 3 2 1

Library of Congress Cataloging-in-Publication Data

The realist's guide to redistricting / J. Gerald Hebert, Paul M. Smith, Martina E. Vandenberg, and Michael B. DeSanctis — 2nd ed.
   p. cm.
   ISBN 978-1-60442-783-7
   1. United States. Congress. House—Election districts. 2. Apportionment (Election law)—United States. 3. Proportional representation—United States. 4. Election districts—United States. I. American Bar Association. Section of Administrative Law and Regulatory Practice.

KF4905.R39 2010   342.73'053—dc22
2009052274

Contents

Foreword

In *Reynolds v. Sims, 377* U.S. 533 (1964), the Supreme Court declared that one person, one vote was the requisite basis for equality in the voting process. In the long electoral history of the United States, severe population disparities in the electoral districts appear to be the norm, not the exception. The decision in *Reynolds* intended to ensure that majoritarian principles would be the primary factor in a state's process of drawing electoral district lines. The decision in *Reynolds,* and in a series of cases exploring issues of voter representation (*see, e.g., Westbury v. Sanders,* 376 U.S. 1 (1964), and *Baker v. Carr,* 369 U.S. 186 (1962)), sought to determine what constituted "fair and effective representation." Though in principle redistricting is intended to protect every citizen's fundamental right to participate in democracy, it is procedurally subject to one of the most political and unpredictable components of our democracy—buffeted by prevailing partisan winds, caprices of state legislators, and a host of complex and evolving issues. This intersection of a fundamental right and political district drawing determines where political party candidates run, who gets to elect them, and thus, who controls state legislative and even congressional seats. Among one of the most controversial issues is to guarantee that historically disenfranchised groups have the right to an effective vote under the Voting Rights Act, 42 U.S.C. § 1971 (2009).

The redistricting process has been the grist of numerous Supreme Court cases addressing questions of population equality, constitutional limits to political gerrymandering, enforcement of Sections 2 and 5 of the Voting Rights Act, and the constitutional parameters to the creation of minority–majority districts. To say the least, the law of redistricting is complex, inconsistent and fact-intensive.

The *Realist's Guide to Redistricting* is a practical handbook about the recondite world of redistricting written by seasoned experts in the field. It is a manual invaluable for practitioners, legislators and citizens who seek to understand the seemingly inscrutable mechanisms that determine the composition of the districts that elect our representatives. The *Realist's Guide* provides the fundamentals of redistricting law and identifies the internal conflicts which make the process so challenging.

The *Realist's Guide* also shows the breadth of administrative law for which the American Bar Association's Section of Administrative Law and Regulatory Practice plays a major role. Administrative law touches all parts of modern life. As Professor Duffy declared, it is about "power, politics, personalities and revolutions in legal thought." (John F. Duffy, "Administrative Common Law in Judicial Review," 77 Texas. L. Rev. 113, 213 (1998).) Redistricting involves everything Professor Duffy describes as administrative law. The Section is proud to be able to publish this second edition of the *Realist's Guide* in time for the 2010 Census and associated redistricting cycle.

> John Hardin (Jack) Young
> Adjunct Professor, Comparative Election Law
> College of William & Mary School of Law
> American Bar Association, Board of Governors

Preface

This is *not* the definitive legal guide to redistricting after the 2010 census. That guide cannot yet be written—at least not without a crystal ball. Some of the most important legal issues that will affect the redistricting process have not been decided by the Supreme Court. In the meantime, the lower courts are "all over the map." Moreover, even those questions that have been decided by the Supreme Court hinge on the vote of a single justice. Today's majority opinion could easily become tomorrow's dissent.

Rather than trying to pretend to be definitive, we offer the *realist's* guide to redistricting.

The realist understands that the very foundations of redistricting law have been shaken to their core in the last couple of decades—both because of deep divisions in the U.S. Supreme Court and because of a lack of consensus among the lower courts about how to balance the delicate issues of race, party, and politics.

The realist understands that arguments that prevail in court, or in one state, or under one set of circumstances, may fall flat when mechanically replicated elsewhere.

The realist understands that a state that zealously seeks to comply with any one of the laws that constrain redistricting—whether it be "one-person, one-vote," the Voting Rights Act, or the "*Shaw* doctrine" —may inadvertently subject itself to liability under another of those laws.

And perhaps, above all, the realist understands that states simply cannot draw districting plans that will go unchallenged in the courts. The best that realistically can be hoped for is to draw plans that will not be *successfully* challenged. At a time when Democrats and Republicans are polarized and—despite the election of the first African-American president in U.S. history—the politics of race and ethnicity remain contentious, the stakes in redistricting are simply too high to avoid litigation altogether. The only realistic goal for a state is to win. And the only alternative to winning is to replace the traditional, once-a-decade redistricting process with a ten-year-long series of skirmishes, each resulting in yet another set of newly reconfigured districts. No one profits from such instability, least of all the voters who will be thrown into a new district before they even get to know the representative of their former district.

This realist's guide, then, is designed to warn the reader of the legal pitfalls that surely lie ahead. States must understand and fully respect each of the legal constraints described in this guide—the "one-person, one-vote" standard, Sections 2 and 5 of the Voting Rights Act, and the constitutional limits on racial and partisan gerrymandering that flow from the Equal Protection Clause of the Fourteenth Amendment. These constraints are invariably in tension with each other—and often with the redistricters' political and partisan goals. A district drawn to satisfy one requirement may violate another. The challenge lies in finding a way to satisfy all these requirements simultaneously. This guide, we hope, will serve as a useful first step.

As should be obvious from the relative brevity of this guide, it is not intended to be a comprehensive treatise on the law of redistricting. We have written this guide to acquaint our readers with the fundamentals of redistricting law—and to identify some of the internal conflicts that make redistricting such a difficult enterprise.

The legal guidelines for proper redistricting have long varied from state to state and from federal court to federal court and, nowadays, they seem to vary from month to month. Only the timely advice of experienced counsel can be relied upon to navigate these ever-changing waters.

Every statewide redistricting plan—whether for Congress or for either house of the state legislature—may be challenged in a three-judge federal district court, with a right to appeal directly to the United States Supreme Court. By statute, the Supreme Court is required to decide these cases, but often it rules on them "summarily," that is, without full briefing or oral argument and often without issuing any written opinion explaining its ruling. Because these summary decisions have limited precedential value, and because the Supreme Court plays such a pivotal role in so many redistricting cases, this field of law is unique. Thus, redistricting counsel must possess not only a realistic understanding of *current* law, but also a nuanced feel for the coming *trends* in the Supreme Court, where shifting majorities and fragile alliances are the norm.

This guide, of course, is by no means intended to present fully such a nuanced, specialized view. It simply is designed to highlight a few of the problems and questions that will face states as they prepare for the post-2010 round of redistricting. We hope you find it helpful.

J. Gerald Hebert
Law Offices of J. Gerald Hebert
Alexandria, Virginia

Paul M. Smith
Michael B. DeSanctis
Martina E. Vandenberg
Jenner & Block LLP
Washington, D.C.

October 2009

Acknowledgments

The authors would like to thank Jessica R. Amunson, Anna M. Baldwin, Joshua A. Block, Eric R. Haren, Nicholas O. Stephanopoulos, Brookes C. Brown, Marina K. Jenkins, and Elisabeth M. Oppenheimer, without whom this guide could never have been written. Cheryl L. Olson, D. Nicole Miller, and Janice K. Skafidas provided superb technical and administrative support. The authors would also like to acknowledge the efforts of those who contributed to the first edition of the *Realist's Guide* in 2000.

About the Authors

J. Gerald Hebert, a sole practitioner in Alexandria, Virginia, specializes in election law and the Voting Rights Act. Gerry spent more than 20 years in the U.S. Department of Justice, where he served in many supervisory capacities, including Acting chief, deputy chief, and special litigation counsel in the Voting Section of the Civil Rights Division. He has taught courses on election law at Georgetown University Law Center, the University of Virginia Law School, and the Washington College of Law at American University. Gerry has authored a number of articles on voting rights and redistricting. From 1999 through 2002, Gerry served as general counsel to IMPAC 2000, the national Democratic Party's congressional redistricting project.

Paul M. Smith, a partner in Jenner & Block LLP's Washington, D.C., office, chairs the firm's Appellate and Supreme Court Practice and co-chairs the Election Law and Redistricting Practice. Paul has argued 13 cases before the Supreme Court, including *Crawford v. Marion County Election Board* (2008), the Indiana voter ID case, and two Congressional redistricting cases, *LULAC v. Perry* (2006) and *Vieth v. Jubelirer* (2003). For nearly two decades, Paul has represented clients in trial and appellate cases involving congressional redistricting and voting rights. Paul graduated from Yale Law School, where he served as editor-in-chief of the *Yale Law Journal*. He clerked for Judge James L. Oakes of the U.S. Court of Appeals for the Second Circuit and for Justice Lewis F. Powell, Jr. of the Supreme Court. He served as a member of the Board of Governors of the District of Columbia Bar and was recognized in the 2007, 2008, and 2009 editions of Washington D.C. *Super Lawyers for Appellate Law* and as one of the Top 100 Lawyers in D.C.

Michael B. DeSanctis is managing partner of Jenner & Block LLP's Washington, D.C., office. He is co-chair of the firm's Election Law and Redistricting Practice, and is a member of the firm's Litigation Department and Creative Content Practice Group. Michael litigated numerous redistricting cases in the 2000 cycle, and has been centrally involved in election law and voting rights cases in the 2004 and 2008 congressional and presidential election cycles. He also maintains an active commercial litigation and copyright practice. His work has extended to the U.S. Supreme Court, the U.S. Courts of Appeals for the District of Columbia, Third, Fourth, Sixth, Eighth, Ninth, and Eleventh Circuits, as well as federal district courts and state courts across the country. In July 2009, Michael was recognized by *The National Law Journal* in its "40 Under 40: Washington's Rising Stars," feature on Washington D.C.'s top lawyers under 40. Michael received his J.D. cum laude from New York University School of Law and his B.A. summa cum laude from Boston College.

Martina E. Vandenberg, a partner in Jenner & Block LLP's Washington, D.C., office, is a member of the Complex Commercial Litigation Practice Group, the Media and First Amendment Practice Group, and the Election Law and Redistricting Practice Group. Martina has represented clients in litigation challenging federal statutes and regulations on First Amendment grounds. She maintains an active commercial litigation practice. Prior to joining the firm, Martina worked at Human Rights Watch, where she conducted policy advocacy and research on war crimes in the Balkans. Martina, a Truman and Rhodes Scholar, was honored with the Albert E. Jenner, Jr. Pro Bono Award for her work representing human trafficking victims and for her legislative advocacy efforts to combat human trafficking. Martina graduated from Columbia Law School, where she was a Harlan Fiske Stone Scholar, and has served as an adjunct faculty member at American University.

CHAPTER 1

Population Equality

Perhaps the most fundamental requirement the law imposes on redistricters is "population equality," also known as the "one-person, one-vote" standard. This principle is captured by the saying "equal representation for equal numbers of people."[1] In practical terms, population equality means that each district in an apportionment plan should have roughly, if not precisely, the same number of people as every other district. There are two different legal standards for determining whether this principle has been satisfied. A rather strict standard, allowing for only the smallest variance among districts, governs congressional redistricting. A considerably looser standard governs all other state and local election districts.

A. MEASURES OF POPULATION (IN)EQUALITY

Before delving into the legal questions, it is important to define two standard measures of population equality. The most widely used measure—the difference between the populations of the most heavily, and the least heavily, populated districts—is called the "overall population deviation" or "total population deviation." Often, this measure is expressed as a percentage of the ideal (or average) population of a district. For example, assume there is a state with 1,000 people and five districts (A, B, C, D, and E). Perfect population equality would result if each of the five districts contained exactly 200 people. The overall or total population deviation would then be zero. But if the redistricting

---

1. Karcher v. Daggett, 462 U.S. 725, 730 (1983) (quoting Wesberry v. Sanders, 376 U.S. 1, 18 (1964)).

plan were altered so that the five districts contained 180, 190, 200, 210, and 220 people, respectively, the deviation would then become quite substantial. The most heavily populated district (District E) would have 220 people, and the least heavily populated (District A) would have 180 people, so the overall population deviation would be 40 people (220 minus 180). Or, expressed as a percentage of the ideal population of a district, the overall or total population deviation would be 20 percent (40 divided by 200).

A second measure of population inequality is "average population deviation," the average of each district's deviation from the ideal. In the above example, District C contained the ideal population (200 people), Districts B and D each differed from the ideal population by 10 persons (190 people or 210 people, respectively), and Districts A and E each differed from the ideal by 20 persons (180 people or 220 people, respectively). Thus, the average deviation would be 12 (the average of 0, 10, 10, 20, and 20), which also can be expressed as 6 percent of the ideal population (12 divided by 200). Courts most often use total population deviation as the yardstick for determining when a deviation is too high to be constitutionally acceptable, but average deviation is sometimes considered as well.

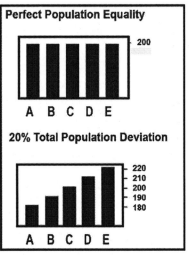

The most common measure of population equality is called "total population deviation" or "overall population deviation."

States engaged in congressional or state-legislative redistricting have ordinarily used the population figures generated by the federal decennial census. In anticipation of the 2000 census, the Census Bureau planned to use forms of the statistical method known as "sampling" to adjust for the chronic problem of differentially "undercounting" certain identifiable groups of individuals, including certain racial and language minority groups, children, and renters.[2] In 1999, the Supreme Court held that the

---

2. *See* Dep't. of Commerce v. U.S. House of Representatives, 525 U.S. 316, 320, 322 (1999).

Census Act prohibited the Bureau's proposed uses of sampling in calculating the "'population for purposes of apportionment of Representatives in Congress among the several States.'"[3] Thus, sampling could not be used in 2000 to determine the size of each state's congressional delegation.[4] But the Court left open the possibility of the use of sampling "for purposes other than apportionment [of congressional seats among the 50 States,] . . . if 'feasible.'"[5]

When the apportionment counts from the 2000 census were delivered to the states, however, the Census Bureau recommended against the use of adjusted data (data drawn from sampling) for redistricting, citing concerns regarding their accuracy.[6] The Secretary of Commerce adopted the recommendation and determined that unadjusted data would be released as the official redistricting data. In October 2001, the Census Bureau director rejected the use of adjusted data even for non-redistricting purposes.[7] Sampling also is not expected to be used in the 2010 census.

The Census Bureau has now separated the tasks of counting residents for apportionment and redistricting purposes from that of collecting detailed socioeconomic information for resource allocation purposes.[8] In 2010, the decennial census will count residents, as well as ask for name, sex, age, date of birth, race, ethnicity, relationship, and housing tenure,[9] while the more detailed information will be collected through a yearly rotation of sampling conducted by the American Community Survey.[10]

---

3. *Id.* at 334, 339–40, 342–43 (quoting 13 U.S.C. § 195).

4. The Census Bureau did use a technique referred to as "hot-deck imputation" to fill in gaps in its information and resolve conflicts in its data. The Supreme Court held in *Utah v. Evans* that this method of supplementing census data did not constitute "sampling" and did not violate the Census Clause. 536 U.S. 452 (2002).

5. Dep't of Commerce, 525 U.S. 316, 339, 341 (quoting 13 U.S.C. § 195).

6. U.S. Census Bureau, History, http://www.census.gov/history/www/through_the_decades/overview/2000.html (last visited Oct. 5, 2009).

7. *Id.*

8. U.S. Census Bureau, Census 2010, http://www.census.gov/acs/www/Special/Alerts/Latest.htm (last visited Oct. 6, 2009).

9. *Id.*

10. *Id.*; U.S. Census Bureau, American Community Survey, http://www.census.gov/acs/www/SBasics/ (last visited Oct. 5, 2009).

B. CONGRESSIONAL DISTRICTS

Section 2 of Article I of the U.S. Constitution, which governs population equality for congressional districts, provides: "The House of Representatives shall be composed of Members chosen every second Year by the People of the several States. . . . Representatives . . . shall be apportioned among the several States . . . according to their respective numbers."[11] The Supreme Court has interpreted this clause to mean that only a very small amount of deviation is acceptable within a state's congressional districting plan.

1. The *Karcher v. Daggett* "Two Step"

The leading case on population equality of congressional districts is *Karcher v. Daggett*.[12] Under *Karcher*, two basic questions must be answered to determine whether a congressional districting plan complies with Article I, Section 2 of the Constitution:

- *First*: Could the population differences among the districts have been reduced or eliminated altogether by a good-faith effort to draw districts of equal population?
- *Second*: If the state did *not* make a good-faith effort to achieve equality, can the state prove that each significant variance among the districts was necessary to achieve some legitimate goal?[13]

As to the first question, a state making a good-faith effort can usually draw congressional districts with virtually no deviations at all. For example, in the 2000s, most states drew plans in which the total deviation was less than 100 people—less than one-fiftieth of 1 percent of the population of an average, or ideal, district.[14] Thirteen states drew plans in which the population of the largest district exceeded that of the smallest district by just *one person*.[15] For example, in North Carolina, 12 districts each had a population of 619,178, and one district had a population of 619,177.[16]

---

11. U.S. CONST. art. I, § 2.
12. 462 U.S. 725 (1983).
13. *Id.* at 730–31.
14. National Conference of State Legislatures, Redistricting 2000 Population Deviation Table, http://www.ncsl.org/LegislaturesElections/Redistricting/RedistrictingPopulationDeviation2000/tabid/16636/Default (last visited Sept. 17, 2009).
15. *Id.*

Thus, one way to avoid any possible constitutional question on the "one-person, one-vote" front is to draw districts with the minimum possible deviation.[17] However, it is not absolutely necessary to do so.

2. Justifying Deviations in a Congressional Plan

Under the second of *Karcher*'s two steps, a state also has the option of enacting a congressional plan with a larger total population deviation, but it must be prepared to prove that *each* significant variance between districts was necessary to achieve some legitimate goal. For example, a state with seven districts could draw five districts containing precisely the ideal number of residents, one district with a significantly higher population, and another district with a significantly lower population—*if* it could prove that the deviations in the latter two districts were directly caused by an effort to achieve some legitimate goal.

That raises the question, Which redistricting goals are considered "legitimate" and therefore capable of justifying a deviation? As long as a state *consistently applies* a legislative policy without discrimination, the following policies *may* justify some variance:

- making districts compact;
- respecting municipal boundaries;
- respecting county boundaries *if* the counties are small enough to represent communities of interest;
- respecting precinct boundaries;
- preserving the cores of prior districts; and
- avoiding contests between incumbents.[18]

---

16. General Assembly of North Carolina, Congress Zero Deviation, http://www.ncga.state.nc.us/GIS/RandR07/Home.html (follow "Congressional" hyperlink; then follow PDF hyperlink for "Ideal versus Actual Populations") (last visited on Oct. 5, 2009).

17. *See, e.g.*, Vieth v. Pennsylvania, 195 F. Supp. 2d 672 (M.D. Pa. 2002) (*Vieth II*), discussed *infra*; *but cf.* Duckworth v. State Bd. of Elections, 213 F. Supp. 2d 543, 551 (D. Md. 2002) (finding a population variance of two persons to be the smallest possible given "the dictates of arithmetic," the limitations of available Census data, and the requirements of the redistricting process), *aff'd*, 332 F.3d 769 (4th Cir. 2003).

18. Karcher, 462 U.S. 725, 740; Abrams v. Johnson, 521 U.S. 74, 98–100 (1997). In *League of United Latin American Citizens v. Perry*, the Supreme Court called into question the legitimacy of incumbency protection as a justification for redistricting decisions in the context of section 2 of the Voting Rights Act. The Court found that a policy of incumbency protection for the

To defend successfully against a population inequality charge, the state must justify its plan by specifically relating *each* overpopulated or underpopulated district to one of those legitimate state policies. In deciding whether a state has succeeded in justifying the deviation, courts weigh several different factors:

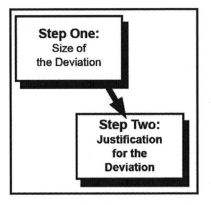

- the size of the deviation;
- the importance of the state's interests;
- the consistency with which the plan reflects those interests overall; and
- the possibility that alternative plans can protect those interests while still maintaining population equality.[19]

The Karcher *"two step" requires states to justify any deviation from perfect population equality in congressional redistricting.*

If the state cannot provide a legitimate justification and specifically relate that justification to *each* overpopulated or underpopulated district, then the apportionment plan probably will be found unconstitutional. That was the case in *Karcher*, where a congressional plan with a total deviation of less than 1 percent (0.6984 percent, to be exact) was not justified by a consistently applied legislative policy.[20]

3. How Large a Deviation Will a Court Actually Approve?

As with so many redistricting issues, it is hazardous to speculate precisely which deviations will be acceptable to the courts and which will be struck down. Significantly, none of the 50 states currently has a congressional districting plan with a total population deviation above 1 per-

---

benefit of officeholders could not justify line-drawing that diminished the voting power of Texas's Latino population. 548 U.S. 399, 441–42 (2006).

19. *See* Karcher, 462 U.S. 725, 741.
20. *Id.* at 728, 742.

cent.[21] But courts have upheld population deviations reaching toward 1 percent in the past, provided the state policies underlying each individual deviation are both legitimate and sufficiently related to the deviation.[22] Nonetheless, only one state currently has a total population deviation above 0.5 percent.[23]

While a state must consistently apply a legislative policy without discrimination, these policies may not be consistently applied or accepted by district courts in different states. The constitutionality of each population deviation must be decided on a case-by-case basis. In its 1997 decision in *Abrams v. Johnson*, the Supreme Court upheld Georgia's congressional districting plan, which had a total deviation of 0.35 percent,[24] in part because the challenged plan's deviations were justified by three legitimate state policies: avoiding split precincts; maintaining communities of interest by not splitting certain counties; and maintaining the cores of prior districts.[25]

The *Abrams* Court expressly reaffirmed, however, that some population variances may be unconstitutional even if they "'necessarily result[ed] from a State's attempt to avoid fragmenting political subdivisions by drawing congressional district lines along existing county, municipal, or other political subdivision boundaries.'"[26] Thus, building congressional districts with whole, undivided counties may justify an otherwise unconstitutional deviation in one plan, or in one state, but not in another. It would be a mistake simply to assume that respect for county lines would *always* prevent a court from invalidating a congressional plan with a high population deviation.[27]

---

21. National Conference of State Legislatures, *supra* note 14.

22. *See, e.g.*, Vera v. Bush, 933 F. Supp. 1341, 1348 & n.9 (S.D. Tex. 1996) (three-judge court); Vera v. Bush, 980 F. Supp. 251, 253 (S.D. Tex. 1997) (three-judge court).

23. Idaho has a total population deviation of 0.60%, with the next-largest deviation reaching only 0.39% in Massachusetts. National Conference of State Legislatures, *supra* note 14.

24. 521 U.S. 74, 99 (1997).

25. *Id.* at 99–100.

26. *Id.* at 99 (quoting Kirkpatrick v. Preisler, 394 U.S. 526, 533–34 (1969)).

27. For example, in 1992 a federal court in Kansas rejected a plan with a total deviation of 0.94% that had been justified only by the goal of retaining the integrity of county lines. State *ex rel.* Stephan v. Graves, 796 F. Supp. 468, 471–73 (D. Kan. 1992) (three-judge court).

4. *Even the Smallest Deviations Must Be Justified*

The state's burden in justifying a population deviation is proportional to the magnitude of the deviation; the greater a state's total deviation, the more compelling the justification must be.[28] States with extremely small deviations still may be required to provide legitimate state policies as justification for any deviation. In 2002, for example, a Kansas congressional districting plan with a total population deviation of 33 persons—equaling 0.0049 percent—survived scrutiny under the "as nearly as practicable" standard by showing the plan's effectiveness in serving the state legislature's legitimate interests: avoiding split counties or voting districts; not diluting minority voting strength; maintaining communities of interest; and prioritizing contiguity and compactness.[29] The court also found it significant that the challenging parties had failed to present a substantially superior plan, though it noted that its province was not "to judge whether the legislature's redistricting choices achieve[d] the *best* possible solution," but rather to determine whether they were "*sufficient* to justify [the] deviation."[30]

In a more straightforward case, a district court in Mississippi found an apportionment plan with a total population deviation of 10 persons (a 0.0014 percent deviation) to "comply fully with the Supreme Court's requirements" as a good-faith effort to achieve perfect population distribution.[31] The court pointed out that in order to achieve absolute perfection, the plan would have had to split precincts, which "would cause administrative problems for election officials and confusion and frustration for voters."[32]

But plans with such small population deviations do not always survive court review. In 2002, a three-judge federal district court in Pennsylvania rejected a congressional districting plan that had a total population deviation of just 19 persons, or 0.0029 percent.[33] The court reasoned that because the Supreme Court "squarely rejected" any *de minimis* exception to the absolute population equality requirement under *Karcher*, and be-

---

28. Vieth II, 195 F. Supp. 2d 672, 677 (three-judge court).
29. Graham v. Thornburgh, 207 F. Supp. 2d 1280, 1295 (D. Kan. 2002) (three-judge court).
30. *Id.* at 1295–97 (emphasis added).
31. Smith v. Clark, 189 F. Supp. 2d 529, 539 (S.D. Miss. 2002) (three-judge court).
32. *Id.* at 539 n.5.
33. Vieth II, 195 F. Supp. 2d 672 (three-judge court).

cause plaintiffs proved a lack of good faith by defendants to avoid the deviation, the variation evidenced a *prima facie* violation of the one person-one vote command.[34] As such, the burden shifted to the state to provide justification for the deviation.

The panel held that the defendants failed to provide any legitimate justification for the population deviations.[35] Even with such a minor deviation, the court found that the justification provided by the defendants—a desire to avoid splitting voting precincts—was a legitimate state interest, but in this case was "a mere pretext."[36] The court further found that the challenged plan failed under *Karcher*'s neutral criteria. Compared with the other maps presented during trial, the challenged plan had the least compact districts, split the most counties, and pitted more incumbents than necessary against one another.[37]

State	Deviation	Decision
Kansas	33 persons	Plan Justified - OK
Pennsylvania	19 persons	Lack of Good Faith; Plan Not Justified - Not OK
Mississippi	10 persons	Good Faith Effort - OK
Maryland	2 persons	Smallest Possible - OK

C. STATE AND LOCAL DISTRICTS

Because Article I, Section 2 of the U.S. Constitution concerns Congress, it is relevant only to congressional redistricting plans. But state legislative districts (and other electoral districts, as well) are also subject to "one-person, one-vote" requirements flowing from the Equal Protection Clause of the Fourteenth Amendment to the Constitution. That clause provides that "[n]o State shall . . . deny to any person within its jurisdiction the equal protection of the laws." In the legislative redistricting context, the Supreme Court has interpreted the clause as requiring states to

---

34. Vieth v. Pennsylvania, 188 F. Supp. 2d 532, 542 (M.D. Pa. 2002) (three-judge court) (Vieth I).
35. Vieth II, 195 F. Supp. 2d 672, 677–78.
36. *Id.* at 677.
37. *Id.* at 678.

make "an honest and good faith effort" to create population equality among districts.[38]

1. The "Ten-Percent Rule"

Even though the words used are similar to *Karcher*'s strict congressional standard, the standard for state legislative districts is far more flexible. A total population deviation of 10 percent or less entitles the state to a rebuttable presumption that the plan was the result of an "honest and good faith effort" to reach population equality among districts.[39] In contrast, a state apportionment plan with a total population deviation above 10 percent creates a *prima facie* case of discrimination, shifting the burden to the state to justify the deviation.[40] Thus, for a hypothetical state with 1,000 residents and five districts, any plan with a total population deviation of 20 persons or less (10 percent of 200) would be presumptively constitutional. But if the total population deviation exceeded 20 persons, the state would be required to justify the variance.

2. Justifying Deviations Above Ten Percent

Apportionment plans for state and local districts are thus given much more leeway than plans for congressional districts. In addition, it may be easier to justify state and local districts with deviations above 10 percent than it is to justify even the most minimal deviation in a congressional districting plan. For example, there is no doubt that preserving political subdivisions is a sufficient justification for deviations in a state or legislative districting plan. On the same day the Supreme Court decided *Karcher*, it also decided *Brown v. Thompson*, upholding a state legislative plan with an average deviation of 16 percent and a total deviation of 89 percent. *Brown* unquestionably marked the outer limits of what might be acceptable in state redistricting plans, and is probably unique because Wyoming's constitution mandates that every county be separately represented in the legislature.[41] The Court upheld the plan because it resulted from a longstanding and consistent application of that legitimate state

---

38. Brown v. Thomson, 462 U.S. 835, 842 (1983) (quotation marks omitted).

39. Daly v. Hunt, 93 F.3d 1212, 1220 (4th Cir. 1996) (quotation marks omitted).

40. Larios v. Cox, 300 F. Supp. 2d 1320, 1339–40 (N.D. Ga. 2004) (three-judge court), *summarily aff'd*, 542 U.S. 947 (2004).

41. Wyo. Const. art. 3, § 49.

policy. However, the Court also noted that providing every political subdivision with a representative would not *always* save an otherwise unacceptable deviation from being struck down.[42] Wyoming's long-standing constitutional policy and its unique geography and demography persuaded the *Brown* Court to uphold the plan, notwithstanding its 89 percent total deviation.[43]

The same rationale, however, was unsuccessful in the litigation over the redistricting plan that followed the 1990 census. Reappraising Wyoming's redistricting plan, which used the same justification the Supreme Court had upheld in *Brown*, the district court found that total deviations of 83 percent in the House plan and 58 percent in the Senate plan were unconstitutionally large.[44] The court stated that Wyoming's state constitutional requirement of county preservation could not be elevated to such an extreme extent over the "one-person, one-vote" requirement of the U.S. Constitution. Instead, the court accepted a revised plan with less than 10 percent deviation for each house.[45] Wyoming again managed to keep the total population deviations of both its House and Senate plans below 10 percent following the 2000 census.

Total Deviation < 10%
Generally, no justification required

Total Deviation > 10%
Justification always required

Apportionment plans for state and local districts also require an "honest and good faith effort" to create population equality across districts. But the standard is far less strict.

As the Wyoming cases suggest, it is crucial to keep in mind not only the federal constitutional requirement of population equality but also state constitutional and statutory districting guidelines. A federal district court in Wisconsin, for example, noted that although it would not always be possible to avoid the division of counties, the prerogatives of the Wisconsin constitution to keep wards and municipalities

---

42. Brown, 462 U.S. 835, 845–46 & n.7.
43. *Id.* at 844–45.
44. Gorin v. Karpan, 775 F. Supp. 1430 (D. Wyo. 1991) (three-judge court).
45. Gorin v. Karpan, 788 F. Supp. 1199 (D. Wyo. 1992) (three-judge court).

whole should be respected when possible.[46] Likewise, the Idaho Supreme Court scrutinized the 2002 state apportionment plan for compliance with the Idaho Constitution, Article III, Section 5, which prohibits the division of counties unless necessary to meet the constitutional standards of equal protection.[47]

In addition to state constitutional requirements, the same justifications used in the congressional context can be used in the state legislative one as well. In 2002, a federal district court in West Virginia upheld a 10.92 percent deviation justified by five state policy interests: recognizing established political subdivisions; compactness; contiguity; maintaining communities of interest; and avoiding crossing county lines unless necessary to preserve the other stated goals.[48] The Supreme Court affirmed.

One potentially important issue that remains unresolved by the Supreme Court is whether there is an absolute limit on population deviation even if the state can demonstrate a legitimate legislative policy. In *Mahan v. Howell*,[49] the Supreme Court upheld a Virginia legislative plan with a total deviation of 16.4 percent, but commented, "While this percentage may well approach tolerable limits, we do not believe it exceeds them."[50] Some lower courts have consequently viewed 16.4 percent as the outer bounds of "tolerable limits" even where a valid justification for the higher deviation exists,[51] though some have allowed greater deviations.[52]

In creating state and local reapportionment plans that satisfy the "one-person, one-vote" standard, then, the key is to keep the total population deviation below 10 percent, if possible, and if the deviation exceeds 10 percent, to justify the excess with consistently applied, nondiscriminatory redistricting policies.

---

46. Baumgart v. Wendelberger, No. 01-C-0121, 2002 WL 34127471, at *3 (E.D. Wis. May 30, 2002) (three-judge court).

47. Bonneville County v. Ysursa, 129 P.3d 1213 (Idaho 2005).

48. Deem v. Manchin, 188 F. Supp. 2d 651, 656 (N.D.W. Va.), *aff'd sub nom.* Unger v. Manchin, 536 U.S. 935 (2002).

49. 410 U.S. 315 (1973).

50. *Id.* at 329.

51. Boddie v. City of Cleveland, 297 F. Supp. 2d 901 (N.D. Miss. 2004) (noting the undisputed presumption that deviations of at least 23.36% and at most 48.7% were in violation of the one-person/one-vote principle); *In re* Apportionment of the State Legislature v. Sec'y of State, 486 N.W.2d 639, 646–47 & nn.36–37 (Mich. 1992).

52. Blackmoon v. Charles Mix County, 386 F. Supp. 2d 1108 (D.S.D. 2005) (upholding a total population deviation of 19.02%).

3. Justifying Deviations Below Ten Percent

The 10 percent rule is not, however, a safe harbor. Rather, it is a threshold that allocates the burden of proof for one-person, one-vote claims.[53] State legislative plans with total population deviations below 10 percent still may be struck down if the population deviation resulted from some unconstitutional, irrational, or arbitrary state policy, such as intentionally discriminating against certain groups of voters, certain cities, or certain regions of the state.[54]

In *Hulme v. Madison County*, for example, a district court in Illinois found that the apportionment process for a local county board, which had a total population deviation of 9.3 percent, was "unquestionably tainted with arbitrariness and discrimination."[55] The court rejected the county board's contention that a plan with a population of less than 10 percent was presumptively valid, and therefore required no justification.[56] Noting that the county board had not offered *any* state policy to justify the population disparity, and, in addition, that the plan was specifically designed to satisfy the political agenda of the chairman of the legislative committee, the court found the apportionment plan unconstitutional.[57]

Similarly, in *Larios v. Cox*, a three-judge panel in Georgia found that the state's legislative apportionment plan, with a total population deviation of 9.98 percent, violated the one-person, one-vote principle.[58] The court acknowledged that while minor deviations may be allowed, these deviations cannot withstand constitutional scrutiny when they are "tainted by arbitrariness or discrimination."[59] Finding that the deviations were not supported by "*any* legitimate, consistently-applied state interests," but were the result of regionalism and partisan gerrymandering, the court struck down the state legislative plan as violative of the one-person, one-vote principle.[60] On appeal, the Supreme Court summarily affirmed.

---

53. Moore v. Itawamba County, 431 F.3d 257, 259 (5th Cir. 2005); Daly v. Hunt, 93 F.3d 1212, 1217–18, 1220–21 (4th Cir. 1996).

54. Moore, 431 F.3d 257, 260; Larios v. Cox, 300 F. Supp. 2d 1320 (N.D. Ga. 2004) (three-judge court), *summarily aff'd*, 542 U.S. 947 (2004).

55. 188 F. Supp. 2d 1041, 1051 (S.D. Ill. 2001).

56. *Id.* at 1052.

57. *Id.* at 1051–52.

58. Larios, 300 F. Supp. 2d 1320, 1352–53.

59. *Id.* at 1338.

60. *Id.* at 1352–53, 1356 (emphasis in original); *cf.* Rodriguez v. Pataki, 308 F. Supp. 2d 346, 370 n.27 (S.D.N.Y. 2004) (distinguishing *Larios* and finding that plaintiffs failed to show that a deviation of 9.78% was not caused by the promotion of court-approved state policies).

D. WHO IS COUNTED

One outstanding issue that remains unresolved by the Supreme Court is what measure of population may be used by states to equalize the population in districts across the state.[61] In *Burns v. Richardson*, the Court said that the Equal Protection Clause does not require the states to use total population figures as the standard by which population equivalency is to be measured.[62] But circuit courts have subsequently interpreted *Burns* in different ways.

In *Garza v. County of Los Angeles*, the Ninth Circuit held that districting based on citizen voting-age population instead of total population would have been unconstitutional.[63] The panel judges disagreed as to which principle lies at the core of one-person, one-vote—the principle of electoral equality, or that of equality of representation. Judges Schroeder and Nelson favored equality of representation, finding for the court that a plan based on citizen voting-age population would impermissibly "dilute the access of voting age citizens in that district to th[eir] representative, and . . . abridge the right of aliens and minors to petition their representative."[64] Judge Kozinski, in dissent, argued that *Burns* "can only be explained as an application of the principle of electoral equality."[65] Viewing the representational equality principle as subservient to the principle of electoral equality, Judge Kozinski argued that individual votes must carry equal weight across districts.[66]

Other circuits have dealt with the question differently. In *Daly v. Hunt* and *Chen v. City of Houston*, the Fourth and Fifth Circuits, respectively, held that the decision as to which population figures to use is a part of the political process, and as such states and localities should be

---

61. Chen v. City of Houston, 532 U.S. 1046 (2001) (Thomas, J., dissenting).

62. 384 U.S. 73, 91–92 (1966). Another controversial issue relating to the proper headcount calculation for purposes of "one-person, one-vote" is where incarcerated individuals are to be counted. The U.S. Census Bureau counts inmates in penal institutions as residents of the institution. *Hayden v. Pataki*, 449 F.3d 305, 329 n.25 (2d Cir. 2006). Since felons and incarcerated persons in many states are barred from voting under state law, this has the effect of increasing the weight of other votes cast in the district.

63. 918 F.2d 763 (9th Cir. 1990).

64. *Id.* at 775.

65. *Id.* at 784 (Kozinski, J., dissenting).

66. *Id.* at 782 (Kozinski, J., dissenting).

given deference.[67] In 2001, the Supreme Court denied a petition for writ of certiorari to hear an appeal of *Chen*. In dissent, Justice Thomas protested that this "critical variable" in the one-person, one-vote requirement has been left undefined.[68] "[A]s long as we sustain the one-person, one-vote principle," he concluded, "we have an obligation to explain to states and localities what it actually means."[69]

---

67. Daly v. Hunt, 93 F.3d 1212, 1227–28 (4th Cir. 1996); Chen v. City of Houston, 206 F.3d 502, 523 (5th Cir. 2000).

68. Chen v. City of Houston, 532 U.S. 1046, 1046 (2001) (Thomas, J., dissenting).

69. *Id.*

CHAPTER 2

The Constitutional Limits on Political (or Partisan) Gerrymandering

Political or partisan gerrymandering refers to the practice of drawing electoral district lines in such a way that one political party benefits and another is disadvantaged. For example, a party's supporters may be "packed" into a few districts where they constitute the overwhelming majority, with the result that the party's share of legislative seats state-wide is substantially smaller than its share of the vote. Similarly, a party's supporters may be "cracked" among several districts so that they do not constitute a majority in any of these districts, with the same consequences for the party's statewide influence. At present, there are no constitutional limits on political gerrymandering, though this may change if the Supreme Court's composition alters or if Justice Kennedy is persuaded that a justiciable standard for measuring partisan gerrymandering can be found.

In the 1986 case of *Davis v. Bandemer*,[1] the Supreme Court held for the first time that political gerrymandering claims *could* be adjudicated by the courts. To prevail on such a claim, a plaintiff had to establish both discriminatory intent, in the sense that districts were deliberately drawn to disadvantage a party, and discriminatory effect, meaning that "the electoral system is arranged in a manner that will consistently degrade a

---

1. 478 U.S. 109 (1986). *Bandemer* focused on Indiana's 1981 Republican-drawn redistricting plan. In the 1982 elections for the Indiana House of Representatives, Democrats received 51.9 percent of the vote but only 43 out of 100 House seats. *Id.* at 115 (plurality opinion).

voter's or a group of voters' influence on the political process as a whole."[2] While *Bandemer*'s intent prong was not particularly difficult to satisfy, its effect prong proved effectively insurmountable over the next 18 years. Not a single plaintiff was ever able to meet both prongs and hence succeed on a political gerrymandering claim.[3]

In 2004, the Court revisited the justiciability of political gerrymandering in *Vieth v. Jubelirer*.[4] Four justices would have overruled *Bandemer* and declared all political gerrymandering claims to be nonjusticiable. In an opinion written by Justice Scalia, they said that *Bandemer*'s approach was "misguided when proposed" and "has not been improved in subsequent application."[5] More fundamentally, in their view, all potential standards for detecting unconstitutional gerrymandering are flawed because they seek to draw an untenable "line between good politics and bad politics."[6] If district-drawers may contemplate political consequences *to some degree*, the plurality observed, nothing in the Constitution can "provide[] a judicially enforceable *limit* on the political considerations that the states and Congress may take into account when districting."[7]

Justice Kennedy, however, concurred only in *Vieth*'s outcome. Like Justice Scalia, he did not consider *Bandemer*'s approach or any of the standards proposed by the *Vieth* litigants or dissenters to be judicially manageable. But unlike Justice Scalia, he was unwilling to shut the door on the possibility that a justiciable standard might subsequently be dis-

---

2. *Id.* at 132 (plurality opinion).

3. *See* Vieth v. Jubelirer, 541 U.S. 267, 279–80 (2004) (plurality opinion) ("[I]n *all* of the cases we are aware of involving that most common form of political gerrymandering, relief was denied."). In one prominent case, California Republicans lost their *Bandemer* claim despite receiving 50.1% of the 1984 statewide vote but only 40% of the congressional seats (18 of 45). *See* Badham v. Eu, 694 F. Supp. 664, 670 (N.D. Cal. 1988), *aff'd*, 488 U.S. 1024 (1989). The court observed that California had a Republican governor and one Republican senator, and remarked that "[i]t simply would be ludicrous for plaintiffs to allege that their interests are being 'entirely ignore[d]' in Congress when they have such a large contingent of representatives who share those interests." *Id.* at 672.

4. 541 U.S. 267 (2004). *Vieth* involved Pennsylvania's 2002 Republican redistricting plan. Republicans won 12 of Pennsylvania's 19 seats in the U.S. House of Representatives in 2002 even though Democrats outnumbered Republicans in the state.

5. *Id.* at 283.

6. *Id.* at 299.

7. *Id.* at 305 (emphasis added).

covered. "That no such standard has emerged in this case should not be taken to prove that none will emerge in the future."[8] Justice Kennedy suggested that a workable test might be formulated on the basis of First Amendment principles rather than the Equal Protection Clause.[9]

The Supreme Court again evaluated a political gerrymandering claim in a 2006 case involving Texas's unusual mid-decade redistricting.[10] In a 5-4 decision, the Court declined to adopt a rule that such mid-decade line-drawing is unconstitutional when motivated solely by partisan objectives. In the majority's view, it is very difficult to determine a legislature's motive for any particular action, and it is not sensible to subject mid-decade redistricting to higher scrutiny than conventional start-of-decade redistricting.[11]

The Court's recent decisions appear to give legislators leeway to pursue partisan advantage as zealously as they like when drawing district lines. Legislators may "pack" or "crack" a party's supporters, ignore traditional districting criteria, create exceedingly safe districts for incumbents, and even redraw lines in the middle of a decade, with some confidence that their decisions will not be second-guessed by courts. Similarly, there is no constitutional requirement of proportional representation of each political party.

As discussed elsewhere in this guide, however, complex constitutional and statutory requirements do apply to redistricting decisions when they involve issues of race and ethnicity. In addition, *state* statutes and constitutions frequently impose limits on political gerrymandering.[12] Furthermore, it is important to note that the Court's two recent political gerrymandering decisions were decided by a plurality and by a slim 5-4 majority, respectively. If a new standard for adjudicating claims of partisan gerrymandering were to emerge that appealed to Justice Kennedy, or if Justice Kennedy were replaced by a justice inclined to agree with the four *Vieth* dissenters, this doctrine could change rapidly and dramatically.

8. *Id.* at 311 (Kennedy, J., concurring in the judgment).
9. *See id.* at 314–17 (Kennedy, J., concurring in the judgment).
10. League of United Latin Am. Citizens v. Perry, 548 U.S. 399 (2006).
11. *See id.* at 416–20.
12. *See* Vieth, 541 U.S. 267, 277 n.4 (citing state laws aimed at "prevent[ing] abusive districting practices" and "insulat[ing] the process from politics").

CHAPTER 3

Section 5 of the Voting Rights Act

Section 5 of the Voting Rights Act, unlike Section 2, applies only to certain parts of the country—specifically, to nine entire states (Alabama, Alaska, Arizona, Georgia, Louisiana, Mississippi, South Carolina, Texas, and Virginia) and to parts of seven others (California, Florida, Michigan, New Hampshire, New York, North Carolina, and South Dakota).[1] Therefore, legislators from the other 34 states need not consider the limits that Section 5 places on the redistricting process. However, for legislators from the "covered jurisdictions," Section 5 remains one of the most significant legal constraints on the redistricting process.

Section 5 requires covered jurisdictions to obtain either administrative preclearance from the Attorney General of the United States or judicial preclearance from the U.S. District Court for the District of Columbia for any change in a "standard, practice, or procedure with respect to voting."[2] A new congressional or legislative redistricting plan—and even a city councilman seat reapportionment plan—qualifies as such a change.[3]

---

1. For a map of all the covered jurisdictions, *see* http://www.usdoj.gov/crt/voting/sec_5/covered.php (last visited Oct. 5, 2009). *See also Procedures for the Administration of Section 5 of the Voting Rights Act of 1965,* 28 C.F.R. § 51.1. Covered jurisdictions are those that "had used a forbidden test or device in November 1964, and had less than 50% voter registration or turnout in the 1964 Presidential election." Northwest Austin Mun. Util. Dist. No. One v. Holder, 129 S. Ct. 2504, 2509 (2009).

2. 42 U.S.C. § 1973c.

3. Beer v. United States, 425 U.S. 130, 133 (1976).

To obtain preclearance, the state must prove that the new redistricting plan does not have the purpose and will not have "the effect of denying or abridging the right to vote on account of race or color, or membership in a language minority group."[4] Thus, Section 5 provides two procedural paths (administrative preclearance by the attorney general and judicial preclearance by the D.C. court) and two substantive standards (commonly referred to as the "purpose prong" and the "effects prong"). States may take either procedural path, but they must satisfy *both* substantive standards. Significantly, a third substantive standard, previously used by the attorney general to deny preclearance to plans that violated Section 2 of the Voting Rights Act, was struck down by the Supreme Court in 1997. Before explaining these points in more detail, it is helpful to understand why Congress enacted Section 5 of the Voting Rights Act.

A THE ENACTMENT OF SECTION 5

The Fifteenth Amendment of the U.S. Constitution, ratified after the Civil War, provides that the "right of citizens of the United States to vote shall not be denied or abridged by the United States or by any State on account of race, color, or previous condition of servitude." The amendment's history suggests it was designed to counter southern states' efforts to prevent newly freed slaves from voting by giving Congress the power to enforce the amendment by appropriate legislation. Pervasive and often violent racial discrimination in voting continued unabated for more than a century.

Congress enacted Section 5 of the Voting Rights Act in 1965. Since then, the Supreme Court has stated that the purpose of Section 5 was to prevent voting-related changes "that would lead to a *retrogression* in the position of racial minorities."[5] Section 5 "was enacted as 'a response to a common practice in some jurisdictions of staying one step ahead of the federal courts by passing new discriminatory voting laws as soon as the old ones had been struck down.'"[6] Effectively, Section 5 "freezes" proposed changes in election procedures in place until the state can prove that the proposed changes are nondiscriminatory in both purpose and effect. If a plan has not been precleared, it is legally unenforceable and

---

4. 28 C.F.R. § 51.52(a); *see also* 42 U.S.C. § 1973c.
5. Beer, 425 U.S. 130, 141 (emphasis added).
6. Reno v. Bossier Parish Sch. Bd., 520 U.S. 471, 477 (1997) (Bossier Parish I) (quoting Beer, 425 U.S. at 140); *see* Miller v. Johnson, 515 U.S. 900, 926 (1995).

may not be implemented. Furthermore, Section 5 places the burden of persuasion squarely on the states: If the evidence is conflicting and the attorney general or the D.C. court is unable to determine whether a new redistricting plan is free of discriminatory purpose and effect, preclearance will be denied.[7]

Rather than designating the jurisdictions to be covered, Congress enacted a formula to determine which states (and political subdivisions) would be "covered jurisdictions." The initial formula, outlined in Section 4 of the Act, provided that a state or political subdivision would be covered by Section 5 if: (1) the state or political subdivision maintained, on November 1, 1964, a "test or device" restricting the right to register or vote;[8] and (2) the Director of the Census determined either that less than 50 percent of the voting age population had registered to vote, or that less than 50 percent of the voting age population had voted in the November 1964 elections.

Congress amended the act in 1970 and 1975, expanding the coverage formula in two key ways. First, Congress covered new jurisdictions based on voting data from the 1968 and 1972 elections, adding those new jurisdictions to those covered by the original formula. And second, Congress significantly expanded the definition of "test or device" to include election-related materials printed only in the English language in states or political subdivisions in which the Director of the Census determined that more than five percent of voting-age citizens are members of a "single language minority."[9] These rules still govern today.

Congress originally intended Section 5 to remain in effect for only five years. However, Congress has reauthorized the statute four times, most recently in 2006.[10] Before the most recent reenactment of the statute, several committees in the House and Senate compiled extensive evidence on the effectiveness of and necessity for the law. The House Judiciary

7. 28 C.F.R. § 51.52(c).
8. Section 4(c) of the act defined a "test or device" as "any requirement that a person as a prerequisite for voting or registration for voting (1) demonstrate the ability to read, write, understand, or interpret any matter, (2) demonstrate any educational achievement or his knowledge of any particular subject, (3) possess good moral character, or (4) prove his qualifications by the voucher of registered voters or members of any other class." 42 U.S.C. § 1973b(c).
9. Section 4(f)(3) of the act has included this expanded definition since the 1975 Amendments. 42 U.S.C. § 1973b(f)(3).
10. *See* Pub L. No. 109-246, 120 Stat. 577 (2006).

Committee held 12 oversight hearings, compiling a record of 12,000 pages.[11] The Senate Judiciary Committee added nine more hearings, collecting another 15,000 pages of testimony and evidence.[12] The committees took testimony from dozens of witnesses, including voting rights scholars, elected officials, and nongovernmental organizations. Congress further relied on the National Commission on Voting Rights' report on its nationwide investigation.[13]

The debate in Congress took several months and even though the extension passed overwhelmingly, there were times when the debate turned contentious. Some House members questioned whether it was appropriate to continue to use data from 1964 to determine which jurisdictions were covered. Others questioned the need for language assistance provisions. In the Senate, members also voiced concerns about the 1964 coverage formula, whether a 25-year reauthorization was too long, and the precise definition of "retrogression" (see Part D below).[14] Despite these concerns, Congress ultimately concluded that "vestiges of discrimination in voting continue to exist,"[15] and the House Judiciary Committee concluded that "there is a demonstrated and continuing need to reauthorize the temporary provisions."[16] Those conclusions were supported by several indicators of continuing and fairly widespread discrimination in voting.[17] In the end, Congress made relatively few amendments to the law, and did not attempt to re-determine the coverage formulas. The amended Section 5 in 2006 passed by a unanimous vote in the Senate and a 390-33 vote in the House. President Bush signed it into law on July 27, 2006.

11. Brief of Reps. John Conyers, Jr., F. James Sensenbrenner, Jr., Jerrold Nadler, and Melvin L. Watt, and Former Rep. Steve Chabot as *Amici Curiae* in Support of Appellees at 17, Northwest Austin Mun. Util. Dist. No. One v. Holder, 129 S. Ct. 2504 (2009), http://www.abanet.org/publiced/preview/briefs/pds/07-08/08-322_AppelleeAmCu3Repsand1FmrRep.pdf (last visted Dec. 11, 2009).

12. *Id.*

13. Northwest Austin Mun. Util. Dist. No. One v. Mukasey, 573 F. Supp. 2d 221, 228–29 (D.D.C. 2008) (quoting H.R. Rep. No. 109-478 (2006)), *rev'd*, 129 S. Ct. 2504 (2009); Nathaniel Persily, *The Promise and Pitfalls of the New Voting Rights Act*, 117 Yale L.J. 174, 179–92 (2007).

14. Nathaniel Persily, *The Promise and Pitfalls of the New Voting Rights Act*, 117 Yale L.J. 174, 183–84 (2007).

15. Pub. L. No. 109-246, § 2(b)(2).

16. H.R. Rep. No. 109-478, at 53 (2006).

17. Northwest Austin Mun. Util. Dist. No. One, 573 F. Supp. 2d 221, 251 (citing several examples included in the legislative history); *see also* H.R. Rep. No. 109-478, at 25-29 (2006).

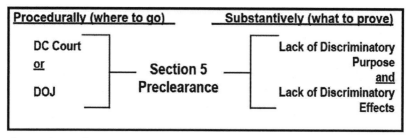

Covered jurisdictions must obtain preclearance for any change in a standard, practice, or procedure with respect to voting.

B. PRECLEARANCE PROCEDURES

As described above, a state (or other covered jurisdiction) has the choice of seeking either administrative or judicial preclearance. The substantive legal standards under either procedure are the same. But a state that has been denied administrative preclearance for a particular plan can seek judicial preclearance for that same plan from the federal court in Washington, D.C.[18] Also, the court in Washington is the only federal district court with the power to preclear a redistricting plan; a federal district court in the redistricted state cannot grant preclearance.

Because administrative preclearance is typically faster and less expensive than litigating in the D.C. court, most states initially seek approval from the attorney general. The Department of Justice has issued federal regulations that set forth at length the procedures for submitting a voting change to the attorney general. Until the *entire* redistricting plan is precleared by federal officials in Washington (either the attorney general or the D.C. district court), *no* part of the plan can actually be implemented by the state.

C. THE "EFFECTS PRONG"

A change in a state's districting plan is considered to have an impermissibly discriminatory effect under Section 5's "effects prong" if it will lead to a "retrogression" in the position of members of a racial or language minority group.[19] "Retrogression" simply refers to any worsening of the position of minority voters. By definition, it requires a "bench-

---

18. *See* Lopez v. Monterey County, 525 U.S. 266, 270–71, 283 (1999).

19. Bossier Parish I, 520 U.S. 471, 487; City of Lockhart v. United States, 460 U.S. 125, 134 (1983); Beer, 425 U.S. 130, 141.

mark" against which one can measure a state's new plan. Normally, the benchmark will be the plan currently in effect when the new plan is submitted for preclearance. If the current plan is an unconstitutional racial gerrymander (discussed below) or is not legally enforceable under Section 5, the last constitutional, legally enforceable plan used by the state will be designated as the benchmark.[20]

Thus, when states redistrict in 2011, the benchmark will generally be the plans that were in effect for the November 2010 elections. Using the most current demographic and political data available, a state will have to make a comprehensive survey of the opportunities for minority group members to exercise their electoral franchise effectively under the old plan. Specifically, a state should assess minorities' opportunities to participate meaningfully in the state's political processes.[21] If a proposed plan

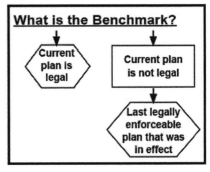

To determine whether a districting plan will lead to "retrogression," the attorney general or D.C. district court uses a prior, constitutional plan as a benchmark.

would lead to a decline in those opportunities, it would likely be denied preclearance on the ground that it had a retrogressive effect.

Central to this inquiry is the question whether minority voting strength would be reduced by the proposed redistricting.[22] Such reductions can take place under at least two entirely different scenarios. *First*, minority voting strength may be reduced by "fragmenting" minority concentrations and dispersing minority voters into two or more districts where they constitute an ineffective minority of the electorate. *Second*, minority voting strength may be reduced by over-concentrating, or "packing," minority voters into one district, or a small number of districts, and thus effectively wasting votes that might have been used to create an additional effective minority opportunity district.[23] Clearly, determining what

---

20. *See* Abrams v. Johnson, 521 U.S. 74, 96–97 (1997); 28 C.F.R. § 51.54(b)(1).
21. 28 C.F.R. § 51.58.
22. *Id.* § 51.59(b).
23. *Id.* § 51.59(c), (d).

constitutes discriminatory fragmenting or packing is a difficult question that implicates fundamental issues about the nature of elections and representation. Congress amended Section 5 in 2006 to make clear that the "purpose" of Section 5 is to "protect the ability" of minority citizens to "*elect* their preferred candidates of choice" (emphasis added).[24]

Many of these same questions and issues are analyzed at length in the discussion of Section 2 of the Voting Rights Act, below. As for Section 5, suffice it to say that these questions and issues will often be subject to legitimate, even heated, dispute, and therefore a state should make precise assessments of minority voting opportunities under both their current plan and various proposed plans *before* finally adopting any plan and most certainly before submitting any plan for preclearance.

The analysis of retrogressive effect becomes even more complex when a state gains or loses a congressional seat due to the post-census reapportionment. In *Abrams v. Johnson*,[25] the Supreme Court addressed the question of whether there is a retrogressive effect when a state's total number of districts increases but the number of minority opportunity districts remains the same. The appellants in *Abrams* unsuccessfully argued that when the size of Georgia's congressional delegation increased from ten seats to eleven following the 1990 census, Section 5 would be violated by any plan that continued to include only one majority-minority district. The Court rejected this contention, stating, "[u]nder that logic, each time a State with a majority-minority district was allowed to add one new district because of population growth, it would have to be majority-minority."[26] The Court has not yet addressed the consequences for retrogression when a state *loses* a congressional seat because of a decrease (or a relatively small increase) in population. That issue may arise after the 2010 census.

---

24. 42 U.S.C. § 1973c(b), (d); *see also* Fannie Lou Hamer, Rosa Parks, & Coretta Scott King Voting Rights Act Reauthorization and Amendments Act of 2006, Pub. L. No. 109-246, § 2(b)(6), 120 Stat. 577, 578 ("The effectiveness of the Voting Rights Act of 1965 has been significantly weakened by the United States Supreme Court decision[] in . . . *Georgia v. Ashcroft*, which [has] misconstrued Congress' original intent in enacting the Voting Rights Act of 1965 and narrowed the protections afforded by section 5 of such Act."); H. Rep. 109-148, at 68–72 (noting that *Georgia*'s holding would lead to results that were "*clearly not* the outcome that Congress intended the Voting Rights Act and Section 5 to have on minority voters" and rejecting the Supreme Court's view) (emphasis in original).

25. 521 U.S. 74 (1997).

26. *Id.* at 97–98.

D. THE "PURPOSE PRONG"

The "purpose prong" of Section 5 asks whether a new districting plan has "the purpose . . . of denying or abridging the right to vote on account of race or color, or [membership in a language minority group]."[27] In January 2000, the Supreme Court in *Bossier Parish II*[28] held that the purpose prong, like the effects prong, focuses entirely on retrogression. Congress overruled this decision by adding section 1973c(c) when it amended and reauthorized the Voting Rights Act in 2006.[29] Thus, a redistricting plan enacted with a discriminatory purpose, even if it is nonretrogressive, will not be precleared.

The Court in *Bossier Parish I* listed several considerations relevant to the purpose inquiry, including:

- the historical background of the state's redistricting decision;
- the specific sequence of events leading up to the enactment of the redistricting plan;
- departures from the normal procedural sequence;
- the legislative history of the plan, especially any contemporary statements by members of the legislature;
- the plan's retrogressive effect, if any; and
- the plan's likelihood of diluting the voting power of minorities.[30]

The Department of Justice's regulations suggest several additional factors that may be relevant to the purpose inquiry, including:

- the extent to which reasonable and legitimate justifications explain the new plan's noteworthy features;
- the extent to which available alternative plans satisfying the state's legitimate governmental interests were considered;

---

27. 42 U.S.C. § 1973c.
28. Reno v. Bossier Parish Sch. Bd., 528 U.S. 320 (2000) (Bossier Parish II).
29. 42 U.S.C. § 1973c(c).
30. Reno v. Bossier Parish Sch. Bd., 520 U.S. 471, 488–89 (1997) (citing Village of Arlington Heights v. Metro. Hous. Dev. Corp., 429 U.S. 252, 266–68 (1977)); *see also* City of Pleasant Grove v. United States, 479 U.S. 462, 469–70 (1987); Busbee v. Smith, 549 F. Supp. 494, 516–17 (D.D.C. 1982) (three-judge court), *summarily aff'd*, 459 U.S. 1166 (1983).

- the extent to which the state followed pre-established, objective guidelines and fair and conventional procedures in adopting the new plan;
- the extent to which the state afforded minority group members an opportunity to participate in the decisions involving the new plan;
- the extent to which the state took the concerns of minority group members into account in formulating the new plan; and
- the extent to which the plan departs from objective redistricting criteria set by the state, ignores other relevant factors such as compactness and contiguity, or displays a configuration that inexplicably disregards available natural or artificial boundaries.[31]

As these lists make clear, the criteria used to evaluate a plan under Section 5's purpose prong are vast and comprehensive. It is thus possible that, even in the absence of blatant "smoking gun" evidence of racism and explicit statements of retrogressive or discriminatory intent, the attorney general (or the federal district court in D.C.) will nonetheless find that a plan cannot satisfy Section 5's purpose prong. Thus, legislators and legislative staffers who in fact act in good faith must nonetheless take care not to leave the impression that their redistricting plans are marred by an impermissible retrogressive or discriminatory purpose.

E. THE CONTINUING CONSTITUTIONALITY OF SECTION 5

The constitutionality of Section 5 was challenged in *Northwest Austin Municipal Utility District Number One (NAMUDNO) v. Holder* in 2009.[32] The case involved a small utility district in Texas that had elected board members. The utility district was founded in 1987, and there was no evidence that it had ever engaged in racial discrimination; however, under Section 5, it was still required to preclear all changes to its election procedures. The utility district challenged the constitutionality of Section 5, and asked in the alternative that it be allowed to "bail out" of the Section 5 preclearance requirements (see discussion below).

The utility district lost before a three-judge panel in the district court, which held that Section 5 was constitutional and that only jurisdictions

---

31. 28 C.F.R. §§ 51.57, 51.59.
32. 129 S. Ct. 2504 (2009).

that registered their own voters (which the utility district did not) could seek a bailout. The case went to the Supreme Court on appeal. After oral argument, many observers doubted that Section 5 would survive, but the Court ultimately decided—in an 8-1 vote—to resolve the case on statutory grounds, interpreting the bailout provision to allow the utility district to seek an exemption from Section 5's requirements.

Section 5 remains valid and applicable to redistricting, but some members of the Court expressed concerns about two issues. First, several members of the Court were skeptical that Section 5 is still necessary, given how few preclearance requests have been denied in recent years. Second, some Justices on the Court expressed concern that the Act still uses voting statistics from 1964 to determine which states are covered and thus subject to the preclearance requirements. These Justices perceived an affront to the sovereign dignity of the covered states.[33] The *NAMUDNO* decision appeared to be an invitation to Congress to update the statute, particularly the determination of which states and portions of states are covered. It is uncertain whether Congress will act on the Court's invitation, and if it does not, whether the Court will strike down Section 5 if given another opportunity.

F. BAILOUT

One important effect of the Supreme Court's decision has been to increase the importance of the bailout provisions of the Voting Rights Act. Section 4(a) of the Voting Rights Act authorizes a "State or political subdivision" to bail out of Section 5's preclearance requirements if the jurisdiction has met a rigorous set of criteria. Specifically, the jurisdiction must show that during the previous ten years,

- no "test or other device has been used within such state or political subdivision for the purpose or with the effect of denying or abridging the right to vote on account of race or color";

---

33. Representatives of the covered states were less concerned. Every senator, including those from the covered states, voted for the 2006 reauthorization. Six covered or partially covered states filed friend of the court briefs in support of the constitutionality of Section 5 in *NAMUDNO*, along with numerous representatives from covered jurisdictions. Only one governor from a covered state filed an opposing brief, and one governor filed a brief in support of neither side.

- "no final judgment of any court of the United States . . . has determined that denials or abridgments of the right to vote on account of race or color have occurred anywhere in the territory";
- "no Federal examiners or observers . . . have been assigned to" the jurisdiction;
- the jurisdiction has complied with the provisions of Section 5;
- "the Attorney General has not interposed any objection (that has not been overturned by a final judgment of a court) and no declaratory judgment has been denied" under Section 5; and
- the jurisdiction has "eliminated voting procedures and methods of election which inhibit or dilute equal access to the electoral process; engaged in constructive efforts to eliminate intimidation and harassment of persons exercising rights protected [by the Voting Rights Act]; and . . . engaged in other constructive efforts, such as expanded opportunity for convenient registration and voting[.]"[34]

Before 2009, this provision was rarely used. The act appeared to limit bailout eligibility to those states or "political subdivision[s]" that actually registered voters. Only 17 such jurisdictions, all in Virginia, had bailed out. However, in *NAMUDNO*, the court held that *all* political subdivisions—meaning, simply, any political division of the state that discharges some governance function—may bail out.[35]

The *NAMUDNO* decision has sparked a new interest in understanding and using the bailout procedures. Indeed, bailout for small entities may become an important part of Section 5 jurisprudence in the coming years.[36]

G. THE RELATIONSHIP BETWEEN SECTION 5 AND SECTION 2

One very important change in Section 5 law occurred in 1997. Previously, the attorney general had a policy of refusing to preclear any plan

---

34. 28 U.S.C. § 1973b(a)(1)(A)–(F).

35. 129 S. Ct. 2504 (2009). Following the decision, the Northwest Austin Municipal Utility District Number One became the eighteenth political subdivision to bail out.

36. Sean Reilly, *Focus: Voting Rights Bailout*, MOBILE PRESS REGISTER, June 29, 2009.

that clearly violated the Justice Department's understanding of Section 2 of the Voting Rights Act—even if the plan was free of discriminatory purpose and effect, as those terms are generally used in Section 5 cases.[37] As discussed below, Section 2 prohibits all jurisdictions from impermissibly diluting the voting strength of minority group members, and uses different substantive standards and burdens of proof than does Section 5. Thus, the attorney general's pre-1997 policy, embodied in a Justice Department regulation that expressly incorporated Section 2 standards into Section 5, significantly increased the attorney general's power to deny preclearance to states' new districting plans. In 1997, the Supreme Court, in *Bossier Parish I*, effectively struck down the Justice Department's regulation when it held that preclearance cannot be denied solely on the basis of a perceived Section 2 violation.[38]

The Court did, however, find that "Section 2 evidence" showing that the new plan dilutes the voting power of minorities may be relevant to whether the jurisdiction acted with a discriminatory purpose under Section 5. Thus, although a plan can no longer be refused preclearance *solely* because of evidence of a Section 2 violation, that evidence may be used to support a finding of discriminatory purpose.[39]

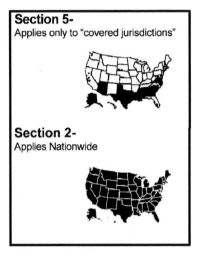

Section 5-
Applies only to "covered jurisdictions"

Section 2-
Applies Nationwide

Unlike Section 2, which applies nationwide, Section 5 of the Voting Rights Act applies only to nine entire states and part of seven other states. Eighteen jurisdictions have "bailed out" of Section 5's preclearance requirements, including 17 jurisdictions in Virginia.

---

37. 28 C.F.R. § 51.55(b)(2) (1997), *removed by* Order No. 2149-98, 63 Fed. Reg. 24,108, 24,109 (1998).

38. 520 U.S. 471, 476–85.

39. *Id.* at 486–90.

CHAPTER 4

Section 2 of the
Voting Rights Act

Section 2 of the Voting Rights Act,[1] unlike Section 5, applies nationwide. Congress passed Section 2 to help effectuate the Fifteenth Amendment's guarantee that no citizen's right to vote shall "be denied or abridged . . . on account of race, color, or previous condition of servitude."[2] In 1982, the act was amended in response to the Supreme Court's decision in *Mobile v. Bolden*, where the Court held that in order to challenge discriminatory voting practices, plaintiffs had to prove intentional discrimination on the basis of race, rather than simply demonstrating that a policy had a racially discriminatory effect.[3] In response to this decision, Congress amended the act to restore a standard allowing liability premised upon discriminatory impact rather than requiring evidence of discriminatory intent.

Section 2 prohibits what is referred to as "minority vote dilution"— the minimization or canceling out of minority voting strength. Section 2(a) of the Act prohibits any electoral practice or procedure that "results in a denial or abridgement of the right of any citizen . . . to vote on account

---

1. 42 U.S.C. § 1973.
2. U.S. CONST. amend. XV.
3. Other factors included evidence such as a history of discrimination, divisive campaign efforts, and the number of minority legislators elected in a region.

of race or color [or membership in a language minority group]."[4] Section 2 (b) specifies that the right to vote has been abridged or denied if,

> based on a totality of circumstances, it is shown that the political processes leading to nomination or election . . . are not equally open to participation by members of a [racial or language minority group] in that its members have less opportunity than other members of the electorate to participate in the political processes and to elect representatives of their choice.[5]

Section 2 thus prohibits any practice or procedure that, interacting with social and historical conditions, impairs the ability of a protected minority group to elect its candidates of choice on an equal basis with other voters.

A. ESTABLISHING A SECTION 2 CLAIM: THE FOUR PRONGS OF *GINGLES* AND *DE GRANDY*

In the context of redistricting, where Section 2 has been applied most frequently, the law poses the following question: When and how must a state draw district lines to avoid diluting the voting power of a protected minority group?[6] Or, more specifically, when must a state create "majority-minority" districts—districts in which a minority group constitutes an effective voting majority?[7]

On its face, Section 2 does not provide a clear framework to answer these questions. In 1986, in *Thornburg v. Gingles*,[8] however, the Supreme Court tried to articulate such a framework. Under the test created in *Gingles*, the first step in determining whether a majority-minority district is mandated by Section 2 is to ask the following three questions:

---

4. 42 U.S.C. § 1973(a).

5. *Id.* § 1973(b).

6. At times, for brevity's sake, this guide refers to a "protected minority group" or a "minority group" or a "minority" as shorthand for a racial- or language-minority group whose members are protected by the Voting Rights Act.

7. As discussed below, there are competing conceptions of an effective voting majority. Courts have not universally accepted any one of these approaches.

8. 478 U.S. 30, 50 (1986).

(1) Is the minority group "sufficiently large and geographically compact to constitute a majority" in a single-member district?[9]
(2) Is the minority group "politically cohesive"?
(3) Does the white majority vote "sufficiently as a bloc to enable it—in the absence of special circumstances...—usually to defeat the minority's preferred candidate"?[10]

If the answer to any of these questions is "No," then Section 2 does not require the state to create a majority-minority district.

A negative answer to first prong of the *Gingles* test means that a minority could not have constituted an effective voting majority in any reasonably drawn alternative district, and therefore the minority's voting preferences could not be satisfied under *any* plan.

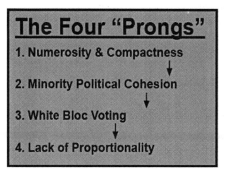

Courts must consider four questions when determining whether a state must create a majority-minority district. Gingles *provides the first three prongs,* De Grandy *provides the fourth.*

A negative answer to either the second or the third prongs means that there is no "legally significant racially polarized voting" to be remedied—either minority voters have not sufficiently coalesced behind a particular set of candidates or white voters have not usually voted to defeat the candidates preferred by minority voters. As the Court has explained, satisfying the first and second prongs together "establish[es] that the minority has the potential to elect a representative of its own choice in some single-member district," and satisfying the second and third prongs together "establish[es] that the challenged districting [plan] thwarts a distinctive minority vote by submerging it in a larger white voting population. . . . Unless these points are established, there neither has been a wrong nor can be a remedy."[11]

---

9. The test enunciated in *Gingles* originally applied only to challenges brought against multi-member districting plans. In 1993, however, the Court made clear that the three-pronged *Gingles* test applies to single-member districting schemes as well. *See* Growe v. Emison, 507 U.S. 25, 40 (1993).
10. Gingles, 478 U.S. 30, 51.
11. Growe v. Emison, 507 U.S. 25, 40–41 (citations omitted).

The *Gingles* requirements do not complete courts' Section 2 inquiries. Even if the answer to all three *Gingles* questions is "Yes," the court must still determine whether, under the "totality of circumstances," the minority group has less opportunity than whites to participate in the political process and to elect representatives of its choice. Only when all these conditions are met must a majority-minority district be created. Although courts have considered a variety of circumstances in making this determination,[12] one factor is particularly important: the "proportionality" or lack thereof, between the number of majority-minority districts and the minority's share of the state's relevant population. It would be very difficult, for example, for a minority group to win a Section 2 case if it constituted 20 percent of the population but effectively controlled 30 percent of the state's districts.

The Supreme Court analyzed the proportionality factor in 1994 in *Johnson v. De Grandy*.[13] The Court assumed for the purposes of deciding *De Grandy* that all three of the *Gingles* factors were satisfied, yet it rejected the plaintiffs' Section 2 claim. As the Court explained, the totality of circumstances did not support a finding of dilution because the "minority groups constitute effective voting majorities in a number of . . . districts substantially proportional to their share in the population."[14] Section 2, in other words, does not mandate that a state create the maximum possible number of majority-minority districts.[15] Although rough proportionality

---

12. For example, courts sometimes consider the following factors, derived from the Senate report accompanying the 1982 amendments to the Voting Rights Act: the extent of any history of official discrimination with respect to the minority's right to vote; the extent to which potentially discriminatory voting practices or procedures, like majority voting requirements or anti–single shot provisions, have been used; if there is a candidate-slating process, whether minority candidates have been denied access to it; the extent of any discrimination against minorities in education or other areas, which might hinder effective participation in the political process; whether political campaigns have been characterized by racial appeals; the extent to which minority group members have been elected to public office; whether there is a lack of responsiveness on the part of elected officials to the minority groups' particularized needs; and whether the policy supporting the use of the voting policy or practice is tenuous. Gingles, 478 U.S. 30, 36–38 (citing Senate Report No. 97-417 (1982)).

13. 512 U.S. 997 (1994).

14. *Id.* at 1024.

15. *Id.* at 1017.

does not automatically protect a state from liability under Section 2, it is a strong "indication that minority voters have an equal opportunity, in spite of racial polarization, 'to participate in the political process and to elect representatives of their choice.'"[16] As Justice O'Connor explained in a separate opinion, proportionality "is *always* relevant evidence in determining vote dilution, but it is *never* itself dispositive."[17]

Although these cases provide a helpful framework for analyzing potential Section 2 claims, many issues concerning the interpretation of Section 2 remain unresolved. Important aspects of these cases were disputed amongst the Justices, and changes in the Court's composition may make it unwise to assume that what has been supported in the past would necessarily receive similar backing today. Even setting aside the changes in the Court's composition, many critical issues have simply never been fully addressed by the highest Court, or have been discussed only in the vaguest terms providing only murky guidance. With respect to the second and third *Gingles* prongs, there are major questions about what constitutes "legally significant racially polarized voting" and what evidence should be used when analyzing it. As for the "fourth prong" enunciated in *De Grandy*, the Court has left open a number of questions relating to the proper measure of "substantial" or "rough" proportionality.

As lower courts have stepped in to fill these voids, they have given different—even conflicting—answers to many of these questions. It is therefore impossible to give a definitive account of what Section 2 requires in every state and in every conceivable circumstance. There is no substitute for consulting the Section 2 case law that applies within one's particular jurisdiction. It is possible, however, to broadly discuss some of the important issues that one should consider when determining whether a plaintiff can bring a viable Section 2 claim.

---

16. *Id.* at 1020 (citing Voting Rights Act, 42 U.S.C. § 1973).

17. *Id.* at 1025 (O'Connor, J., concurring). In LULAC, the Court reaffirmed that proportionality mitigates against finding a Section 2 violation, while making clear that the proportionality inquiry does not allow a state to "trade off the rights of some members of a racial group against the rights of other members of that group." LULAC, 548 U.S. 399, 437. LULAC holds that the appropriate question under Section 2 is not whether the line-drawing in a plan as a whole dilutes minority voting strength, but whether the line-drawing as to particular districts challenged under that plan dilutes minority voting strength. In other words, the proportionality inquiry does not allow a state to remedy vote-dilution injuries suffered by minorities in one part of a state simply by creating a majority-minority district elsewhere in the state.

B. THE FIRST PRONG OF THE *GINGLES* TEST

The first prong of the *Gingles* test asks whether a minority group is "sufficiently large and geographically compact to constitute a majority" in an alternative single-member district.[18] Consequently, there are two important issues related to the first prong: *numerosity* (in other words, the definition of "sufficiently large") and *geographical compactness.* Although these two issues may in some circumstances be interrelated, they raise distinct legal complications.

1. Numerosity

At first glance, the question whether a minority population is "sufficiently large" to constitute a majority in an alternative single-member district seems as if it would be relatively simple to answer. In order to determine the size of a population, however, one must first answer two threshold questions:

- *First,* what is the proper population base—or denominator—that one should use to make the calculation? Should one use the total population of the hypothetical district or some subset of that figure, like voting-age population or the population of *citizens* of voting age?
- *Second*, what percentage of the proper population base constitutes a "majority" for these purposes? Must the minority group simply exceed 50 percent of the given population base, or must it constitute an "effective" voting majority that can actually elect its preferred candidate?

While recent Supreme Court decisions provide significant guidance on these questions, the lower courts retain discretion in choosing the figures that they will use.

a. The Denominator: What Is the Proper Population Base?

There is a wide variety of population bases that courts might use—and have used—to evaluate whether a minority group constitutes a majority

---

18. Gingles, 478 U.S. 30, 50.

in a district. The options include the total population, the voting-age population (VAP), the population of *citizens* of voting age (CVAP), the population of registered voters, the population of actual voters who turned out in a recent election or set of elections, the population adjusted for growth since the most recent census, and the population adjusted for the alleged undercounting of minorities.

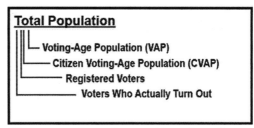

Of course, selecting one of these methods over another can drastically alter the results and have a dispositive effect on the viability of a plaintiff's claims. In *McNeil v. Springfield Park Dis-*

Courts may choose from a wide variety of population bases in answering the question of whether a minority population is "sufficiently large" to constitute a majority in a district.

trict,[19] for example, the Court of Appeals for the Seventh Circuit rejected a Section 2 claim where blacks comprised only 43.7 percent of the voting age population in the plaintiffs' proposed remedial district, even though 50.4 percent of the district's total population was black. As the court explained in its decision, the first prong of the *Gingles* test "roughly measures minority voters' potential to elect candidates of their choice. Because only minorities of voting age can affect this potential, it is logical to assume that the Court intended the majority requirement to mean a voting age majority."[20] Likewise, in *Brewer v. Ham*, the Court of Appeals for the Fifth Circuit explained that because only persons of voting age can vote, "[i]t would be a Pyrrhic victory for a court to create a single-member district in which a minority population dominant in absolute, but not in voting age numbers, continued to be defeated at the polls."[21]

The Supreme Court has not directly resolved which of these population bases should be used in establishing a Section 2 claim,[22] and its opinions have provided mixed signals. In *LULAC v. Perry*,[23] the Court

---

19. 851 F.2d 937 (7th Cir. 1988).

20. *Id.* at 945.

21. Brewer v. Ham, 876 F.2d 448, 452 (5th Cir. 1989) (quotation marks omitted).

22. *See* De Grandy, 512 U.S. 997, 1008–10 (expressly declining to decide this question).

23. LULAC, 548 U.S. 399, 429.

avoided formally ruling on the broader issue. But the Court did appear to endorse using a population base of voting-age citizens (CVAP). In finding that a proposed plan would not count as an opportunity district (a district where minority voters have the capacity to elect a candidate of their choice), the Court noted that "Latinos to be sure, are a bare majority of the voting-age population . . . but only in a hollow sense, for the parties agree that the relevant numbers must include citizenship. This approach fits the language of Section 2 because only eligible voters affect a group's opportunity to elect candidates."[24] The Court appeared to employ a different standard in the more recent case of *Bartlett v. Strickland*,[25] where the majority opinion consistently referred to voting age population (VAP) without reference to citizenship.[26]

Before the *LULAC* and *Bartlett* decisions, however, a few lower courts had used the overall minority population in assessing the first *Gingles* prong.[27] But, consistent with the Supreme Court's recent decisions, courts will likely use either VAP or CVAP as a measure of a group's population base in deciding claims under Section 2 of the Voting Rights Act. As between VAP and CVAP, where there is a considerable difference between the two figures, the *LULAC* decision suggests that courts should use the more meaningful number incorporating citizenship rates.[28] Some lower courts have long adhered to this rule. For example, in *Cano v. Davis*, the U.S. District Court for the Central District of California noted that "the purpose of the first *Gingles* pre-condition is to determine whether minority voters have the *potential* to form an effective majority district; because non-citizens cannot register to vote . . . they should not be included in the figures used to determine whether an additional district can be drawn in which the minority group would have sufficient voting power to elect an additional representative of choice."[29] This issue will likely be in the forefront of post-2010 redistricting litigation.

---

24. *Id.*
25. 129 S. Ct. 1231 (2009).
26. *Id.* at 1250 (Souter, J., dissenting).
27. *See, e.g.*, New Rochelle Voter Defense Fund v. City of New Rochelle, 308 F. Supp. 2d 152 (S.D.N.Y. 2003).
28. LULAC, 548 U.S. 399, 429.
29. Cano v. Davis, 211 F. Supp. 2d 1208, 1233–34 (C.D. Cal. 2002) (citing Romero v. City of Pomona, 883 F.2d 1418 (9th Cir. 1989)), *aff'd*, 537 U.S. 1100 (2003); Meza v. Galvin, 322 F. Supp. 2d 52 (D. Mass. 2004); Chen v. City of Houston, 206 F.3d 502 (5th Cir. 2000); Negron v. City of Miami Beach, 113 F.3d 1563, 1568 (11th Cir. 1997); Campos v. City of Houston, 113 F.3d 544, 548 (5th Cir. 1997). *But see* Barnett v. City of Chicago, 969 F. Supp. 1359,

b. The Numerator: When Is the Minority Group "Sufficiently Large"?

The first prong of the *Gingles* test asks whether the minority group is "sufficiently large . . . to constitute a [] majority" in a district. But the *Gingles* Court also repeatedly referred to "effective voting majorit[ies]"[30] As a result, there has been some disagreement among lower courts as to the proper definition of "majority" for purposes of *Gingles'* first prong. Can a group constitute an "effective voting majority" even if it accounts for less than 50 percent of the population in a district? Conversely, can a group account for more than 50 percent of the population but still not constitute an "effective voting majority" capable of electing their preferred candidates over the opposition of most of the white voters in the district?

The Court answered the first question in *Bartlett v. Strickland*.[31] Resolving a question that had divided the lower courts for many years, the Court held that in order to satisfy the first *Gingles* factor, a minority group must constitute more than 50 percent of the voting-age population in a proposed majority-minority district. Concerned with developing a judicially manageable standard, the Court held that only upon reaching the 50 percent mark could a minority population qualify as a group capable of electing a candidate of its choice. The Court, with Justice Kennedy writing for the majority, held that "the majority-minority rule relies on an objective, numerical test: Do minorities make up more than 50 percent of the voting-age population in the relevant geographic area? This rule provides straightforward guidance to courts and to those officials charged with drawing district lines to comply with Section 2."[32]

As a result, if a minority group constitutes less than 50 percent of the population in a hypothetical district, it cannot prevail on a Section 2 claim, even if the group would be able to regularly elect the candidate of its choice with the reliable support of "cross-over" white voters. Under

---

1421 (N.D. Ill. 1997) (rejecting CVAP as a "methodological quagmire"), *aff'd in part and vacated in part,* 141 F.3d 699 (7th Cir. 1998).

30. *See* Thornburg v. Gingles, 478 U.S. 30, 38.

31. Bartlett v. Strickland, 129 S. Ct. 1231 (2009).

32. *Id.* at 1245.

Bartlett, while legislators remain permitted to draw such cross-over districts, they are not required by the Voting Rights Act to do so.[33]

Bartlett made clear that a numerical majority is a necessary condition for satisfying *Gingles'* first prong, but it did not resolve the question of how much beyond a mere numerical majority-minority voters must be in a district in order to elect their candidate of choice. If, for example, white voters are more cohesive than black voters, the threshold for an effective majority could be substantially greater than 50 percent. As one court explained, an opportunity district is "one in which a black majority has a practical opportunity to elect the candidate of its choice. A simple majority is not always sufficient to provide this opportunity."[34]

A numerical majority may also fail to be an "effective" majority if the population is based on some criteria other than actual voters. Assume, for example, that whites and blacks are equally cohesive, but that a higher percentage of blacks are not registered to vote, have higher non-voting age percentages, or are unable to make it to the polls on Election Day. Under these circumstances, blacks may account for more than half the voting age population in a district, yet the actual electorate may be majority white and capable of regularly defeating black-preferred candidates. Courts receptive to this argument have evaluated minority voting strength using adjusted figures: beginning with a simple majority (50 percent plus one voter) and adding 5 percent for lower turnout, 5 percent for lower voter registration figures, and 5 percent for the larger number of non-voting age residents. This yields an adjusted required majority of 65 percent, using total population as the denominator.[35] Where data on voting age population is available, some

---

33. Similarly, in *LULAC v. Perry* the Court found that influence districts are not required by Section 2. These districts are areas where a minority group, although too small to control an election, is of sufficient size to "influence" the politics of the district in some way or to influence the representative who will ultimately be elected from the district, even though most members of the minority group will have voted against that representative. The Court found that "while the presence of districts 'where minority voters may not be able to elect a candidate of choice but can play a substantial, if not decisive, role in the electoral process' is relevant to the § 5 analysis, the lack of such districts cannot establish a § 2 violation." LULAC, 548 U.S. 399, 446 (internal citations omitted).

34. African Am. Voting Rights Legal Defense Fund, Inc. v. Villa, 54 F.3d 1345, 1348 n.4 (8th Cir. 1995).

35. Ketchum v. Byrne, 740 F.2d 1398, 1413 (7th Cir. 1984).

courts have used 60 percent of the VAP as the basis to analyze minority voting strength.[36] These standards have never been litigated before the Supreme Court, and, at least in this rough form, may be obsolete in the face of increasingly sophisticated data.

2. Compactness

In addition to asking whether a minority group is "sufficiently large," the first prong of the *Gingles* test also asks whether a minority group is "sufficiently . . . geographically compact" to constitute a majority in a new district. In *LULAC v. Perry,*[37] the Supreme Court clarified that *Gingles'* compactness requirement applies to plaintiffs and states alike. As part of a challenged redistricting plan, Texas had dismantled a pre-existing, geographically compact majority-minority Latino congressional district, and replaced it with a district that stretched more than 300 miles that combined two geographically separated groups of Latinos with divergent needs and interests. *LULAC* held that, just as a minority group must demonstrate they are sufficiently large and geographically compact to constitute a majority in a district, a state similarly cannot dismantle a compact majority-minority district and remedy the Section 2 violation by replacing it with "a district that combines two far flung segments of a racial group with disparate interests."[38]

For some time, there have been two competing definitions of compactness. Some advocates think of "compactness" as a question of geometry. These advocates, whether they use a mathematical formula or they "eyeball" it, analyze a district's compactness in terms of its shape on a map. In particular, they are likely to focus on the regularity or jaggedness of the district's edge and the degree to which the district's territory is dispersed around its center. The smoother a district's border, and the more its shape resembles a square or a circle rather than a spider or a string bean, the more likely it will be deemed "compact" under this view.

Others take a more "functional" approach to compactness, which analyzes the distribution of a district's population in relation to such

36. *See* Campuzano v. Ill. State Bd. of Elections, 200 F. Supp. 2d 905, 910 (N.D. Ill. 2002); Jeffers v. Clinton, 756 F. Supp. 1195, 1198–99 (E.D. Ark. 1990), *aff'd*, 498 U.S. 1019 (1991); United States v. Euclid City School Bd., 632 F. Supp. 2d 740, 768–69 (N.D. Ohio 2009).
37. League of United Latin American Citizens v. Perry, 548 U.S. 399 (2006).
38. *Id.* at 433.

features as topography (mountain ranges, rivers, bays, etc.), lines of communication and transportation, recognized neighborhoods, and local government boundaries. This approach asks whether candidates or legislators could explain to their constituents the boundaries of their districts in simple, common-sense terms, based on recognizable geographic referents. An example might be a district containing a particular and easily recognized part of a county with discernable borders. Under a functional notion of compactness, the question is not whether the district is aesthetically pleasing when viewed "vertically" (as on a map), but whether it makes sense to the person on the street, looking "horizontally."

Compactness is measured differently in Section 2 cases than in racial-gerrymandering cases brought under the Fourteenth Amendment. In racial-gerrymandering cases, the Court has at times referred to geometric shape and objective measures of jaggedness and dispersion, and at other times focused on whether the use of race subordinated other more functional concerns, such as respect for city and county lines and for recognizable communities of interest.[39] But *LULAC* held that—unlike the racial-gerrymandering cases, which focus on the shape of the district— the "first *Gingles* condition refers to the compactness of the minority population, not to the compactness of the contested district."[40]

The Court in *LULAC* noted that "no precise rule has emerged governing Section 2 compactness" but emphasized the need to recognize several of the non-geographic factors.[41] For example, the Court emphasized the importance for compactness of shared political and cultural interests in addition to geographic concerns. Seeking to avoid racial essentialism—the idea that members of a particular minority group automatically share identical views—the Court noted that there are divergent interests even within groups that are racially or ethnically homogenous. Justice Kennedy declared that if the Court did not account for the differences between people of the same race it would do a disservice to the Voting Rights Act's dual goals of preventing electoral discrimination and "foster[ing] our transformation to a society that is no longer fixated on race."[42] In deciding that one of the challenged majority-minority districts could not remedy a Section 2 violation, the *LULAC* majority "emphasize[d]" that it was not only the

---

39. See the discussion in Chapter 5 on compactness in the context of *Shaw*-type racial gerrymandering claims.
40. 548 U.S. 399, 433 (quotation marks omitted).
41. *Id.*
42. *Id.* at 434 (citing Georgia v. Ashcroft, 539 U.S. 461, 490 (2002)).

"enormous geographical distance" separating two communities that had been joined together, but also "the disparate needs and interests of these populations—not either factor alone—that renders [the challenged district] noncompact for Section 2 purposes."[43]

The compactness standard of the first *Gingles* prong, therefore, includes both geographic factors, traditional non-geographic components like historical boundaries and man-made elements, and an awareness of communities of interest, even within recognized minority groups. In practice, it is possible the cultural and political concerns will largely be swallowed by geographic considerations, but where such cleavages exist within minority communities, they may prove important.

C. THE SECOND AND THIRD PRONGS: RACIALLY POLARIZED VOTING

The second and third prongs of the *Gingles* test—minority political cohesiveness and white bloc voting—together form the inquiry into racially polarized voting. Racial polarization exists, the Court explained in *Gingles,* "where there is a consistent relationship between [the] race of the voter and the way in which the voter votes . . . or to put it differently, where black voters and white voters vote differently."[44] Although the first prong of the *Gingles* test is critical, racially polarized voting has been described as the "linchpin" and the "true test" of vote dilution claims.[45] If there is no racially polarized voting, "it cannot be said that the ability of minority voters to elect their chosen representatives is [less than] that of white voters."[46]

1. Statistical Methods for Identifying Racially Polarized Voting

The inquiry into racially polarized voting typically entails the use of complex statistical analysis. Traditionally, courts relied upon two statistical methods to examine the question of polarization: "homogeneous precinct analysis" and "bivariate ecological regression analysis." In recent years, courts have begun to adopt a third method: "ecological in-

---

43. *Id.* at 435.
44. Gingles, 478 U.S. 30, 53 n.21 (internal quotation marks omitted; bracket in original).
45. *Id.* at 93 (O'Connor, J., concurring in the judgment).
46. *Id.* at 48 n.15

ference," sometimes referred to as "King's EI."[47] Each of these methods allows experts, using aggregate data, to draw certain conclusions about voting preferences of groups of voters—specifically, how members of particular racial or ethnic groups cast their ballots. Because the secret ballot prevents the tabulation of electoral data at the individual level, voting behavior typically must be inferred from precinct-level electoral data.

Homogeneous precinct analysis is simply the tallying of votes cast in precincts overwhelmingly populated by members of one racial or ethnic group. For example, one could get some idea of how white voters are voting by looking only at overwhelmingly white precincts, and one could then do the same for overwhelmingly black or Hispanic precincts. If, to take one extreme and entirely hypothetical example, everyone in a state lived in an all-white, an all-black, or an all-Hispanic precinct, one could simply add up the results of each of these three types of precincts and achieve a perfect understanding of how members of the three different groups voted. Conversely, if everyone in the state lived in a precinct in which the racial and ethnic composition was precisely the same as the statewide average, it would be impossible to draw any conclusion about the voting behavior of whites, blacks, and Hispanics by conducting a homogeneous precinct analysis.

Of course, in reality, every jurisdiction is somewhere in between— neither perfectly segregated nor perfectly integrated. Therefore, political scientists and other experts typically use a more sophisticated form of analysis, known as bivariate ecological regression analysis, to estimate voting behavior by race. Like homogeneous precinct analysis, bivariate ecological regression discerns relationships between the racial composition of voting precincts and the total votes cast for each candidate in those precincts. Unlike homogeneous precinct analysis, it takes into consideration data from all precincts, not just those that are overwhelmingly populated by members of one racial or ethnic group.

Though many courts have continued to rely upon a combination of homogenous precinct analysis and ecological regression,[48] and some courts (including the Supreme Court) appear in some cases to have used only

---

47. In reference to the method's originator, Harvard professor and statistician Gary King.

48. *See, e.g.,* Rodriguez v. Bexar County, 385 F.3d 853, 865–66 (5th Cir. 2004); United States v. Blaine County, 363 F.3d 897, 915 n.27 (9th Cir. 2004); Rural W. Tenn. African Am. Affairs Council v. Sundquist, 209 F.3d 835, 839 (6th Cir. 2000).

regression or only ecological inference,[49] many courts have moved to relying upon a combination of all three statistical methods. Several courts have found evidence gleaned from using all three of these methods more convincing than that produced by using only one.[50] Courts have avoided adopting a strict guideline for the use of these methodologies, both for selecting amongst them and in acting upon the statistical conclusions they produce. As one court stated:

> It is important to keep in mind . . . that the court's job is to assess the broader legal principles described in *Gingles*; it is neither to be wedded to, or hamstrung by, blind adherence to statistical outcomes. Statistics are tools to aid the Court's analysis. There are no bright line absolutes to which this Court must adhere in assessing the question of whether racial bloc voting existed...As a result, while courts have found certain particular statistical or mathematical outcomes to be compelling evidence *in the context of the cases before them,* no decision out of either the Supreme Court or the Sixth Circuit (or any other Circuit for that matter) requires the use of a particular statistical methodology, or demands a particular statistical outcome before a court may conclude that racial bloc voting exists.[51]

In the absence of strict guidelines, these methods often are the subject of contentious litigation and "battles of the experts."

---

49. *See, e.g., LULAC*, 548 U.S. 399, 467; Old Person v. Cooney, 230 F.3d 1113, 1122–27 (9th Cir. 2000) (using only regression); Cottier v. City of Martin, 466 F. Supp. 2d 1175 (D.S.D. 2006) (appearing to use only ecological inference).

50. *See* Levy v. Lexington County, No. 03-3093, 2009 U.S. Dist. LEXIS 13385 (D.S.C. Feb. 19, 2009) (noting that the court found the use of homogeneous precinct, ecological regression, and ecological inference [EI] more reliable than analysis using EI alone); United States v. City of Euclid, 580 F. Supp. 2d 584, 598 (N.D. Ohio 2008) (endorsing an expert's view that "while King's EI method is an improvement upon HPA [homogeneous precinct analysis] and BERA [bivariate ecological regression analysis], it does not replace these two traditional methods. Instead, experienced political scientists use all three methods, not only to estimate voting behavior, but as a method for cross-checking the reliability of estimates.").

51. 580 F. Supp. 2d 584, 596.

Aside from these methodological matters, there are a host of important questions relating to the racially polarized voting inquiry for which courts have given varied and inconsistent answers. Courts have often used statistical findings as a place to commence their analysis rather than relying on those findings to reach a conclusion. Anecdotal evidence is often used to supplement statistical findings.[52]

2. What Is "Minority Political Cohesiveness"?

Courts have voiced some disagreement with respect to what constitutes "minority political cohesiveness" under *Gingles'* second prong. In *Gingles*, the Supreme Court declared that one purpose of the inquiry into racially polarized voting is "to ascertain whether minority group members constitute a politically cohesive unit. . . . A showing that a significant number of minority group members usually vote for the same candidates," the Court explained, "is one way of proving the political cohesiveness necessary to a vote dilution claim."[53]

Following this suggestion from the Supreme Court, most lower courts have limited their political-cohesiveness inquiries to a study of voting patterns. As the Court of Appeals for the Ninth Circuit stated in *Gomez v. City of Watsonville*,[54] an inquiry into political cohesiveness should be directed at "whether the minority group has expressed clear political preferences that are distinct from those of the majority" and should be "judged primarily on the basis of the voting preferences expressed in actual elections."[55] An indication of minority cohesion exists when there has been sustained minority support for candidates in past elections, though courts sometimes disagree on whether support for minority candidates warrants special attention.

Although many courts rely on statistical evidence of voting patterns,[56] others have stated that the inquiry into cohesiveness "'does not stop with

---

52. *See, e.g., id.* at 600–01; Whitfield v. Democratic Party of Ark., 890 F.2d 1423, 1428 (8th Cir. 1989); Rural W. Tenn., 209 F.3d 835, 844; Askew v. City of Rome, 127 F.3d 1355, 1377 (11th Cir. 1997).

53. Gingles, 478 U.S. 30, 56; *see also* Jamison v. Tupelo, 471 F. Supp. 2d 706 (N.D. Miss. 2007); Bone Shirt v. Hazeltine, 336 F. Supp. 2d 976 (D.S.D. 2004).

54. 863 F.2d 1407 (9th Cir. 1988).

55. *Id.* at 1415.

56. Bone Shirt v. Hazeltine, 336 F. Supp. 2d 976 (D.S.D. 2004) (proving this factor typically requires statistical evaluation of elections).

bare statistics.'"[57] A few courts have been willing to entertain evidence beyond voting preferences to determine whether a minority group has distinctive group interests.[58] In *Sanchez v. Bond*,[59] for instance, the Court of Appeals for the Tenth Circuit affirmed a district court's finding that Hispanics in Saguache County, Colorado, were not politically cohesive. Although statistical evidence indicated that voting was racially polarized, the district court relied on testimony by a single lay witness that Hispanics had "differing political objectives."[60] As the court explained, there is "nothing in *Gingles* . . . to suggest that a trial court is *prohibited* from considering lay testimony in deciding whether a minority group is politically cohesive."[61] Another court has held that "[e]vidence that 'a specified group of voters share common beliefs, ideals, principles, agendas, concerns, and the like such that they generally unite behind or coalesce around particular candidates and issues, demonstrates cohesion.'"[62]

Complicating matters further, there is some disagreement—even among courts that focus solely on election data—about what level of voting alignment constitutes political cohesiveness. The Supreme Court's use of the term "significant number" in *Gingles* did not clarify matters much. Courts face many of the same problems in this assessment that, as we will discuss below, plague them in evaluating minority preferred candidates. Some courts, for instance, have required a showing that 60 percent of minority group members vote together for the same candidates in a two-way race; other courts have not adopted such a standard.[63] When there are three or more candidates in the field, the issue becomes more complicated, and courts have not reached consensus on how best to determine minority political cohesion in such contests.

Similarly, the question of political cohesiveness is significantly more complicated in regions with more than one minority group. In these cases,

---

57. *Id.* at 1004 (quoting Whitfield, 890 F.2d at 1428).

58. *See* Monroe v. City of Woodville, 881 F.2d 1327, 1331 (5th Cir. 1989); Houston v. Haley, 859 F.2d 341, 346 (5th Cir. 1988).

59. 875 F.2d 1488 (10th Cir. 1989).

60. *Id.* at 1496.

61. *Id.* at 1493.

62. Bone Shirt, 336 F. Supp. 2d 976, 1004 (quoting League of United Latin Am. Citizens, Council No. 4434 v. Clements, 986 F.2d 728, 744 (5th Cir. 1993)); *see also* Askew NAACP v. City of Rome, 127 F.3d 1355, 1377 (11th Cir. 1997) (both empirical and anecdotal evidence demonstrated cohesion).

63. *See, e.g.,* Marylanders for Fair Representation, Inc. v. Schaefer, 849 F. Supp. 1022, 1056 (D. Md. 1994) (three-judge court).

courts have grappled with the question of what kind of evidence must be shown to prove that the two different minority groups—African-Americans and Hispanics, for example—are politically cohesive not only internally, but also with each other. As in other areas, courts have reached differing conclusions regarding cohesiveness between minority groups.[64]

3. What Evidence Does a Court Use to Determine Racial Polarization?

Courts also have failed to reach a consensus about what data set to use when evaluating the degree of racial polarization in a community. In determining whether a white majority votes sufficiently as a bloc "to enable it . . . usually to defeat the minority's preferred candidate," it is necessary first to answer several preliminary questions, including: how to determine the minority's preferred candidate (specifically, whether the races of the candidates are relevant), whether to examine elections for offices other than the one at issue, and how many past elections should be considered. These questions are crucial in Section 2 cases because their answers will often dictate the conclusions reached. As one court put it in discussing the plaintiffs' and defendants' experts: "Their conclusions differed because of the differences in the statistical evidence they chose to evaluate."[65]

a. How Does One Determine the Minority-Preferred Candidate?

To determine whether minority-preferred candidates are usually defeated, it is necessary first to determine the identity of the minority-preferred candidates. As one court has stated, "[a]scertaining whether legally significant white bloc voting exists begins with identification of the minority members' 'preferred candidates' or 'representatives of choice.'"[66] In identifying the preferred candidate, courts have taken different approaches on two key issues. *First,* courts have not agreed on whether a candidate's

64. Samuel Issacharoff, *Groups and the Right to Vote*, 44 EMORY L.J. 869, 886 n.81; LULAC v. Perry, 548 U.S. 399 (2006); Note, *The Ties That Bind: Coalitions and Governance Under Section 2 of the Voting Rights Act*, 117 HARV. L. REV. 2621, 2629 (2004); Campos v. City of Baytown, 840 F.2d 1240, 1244–45 (5th Cir. 1988).

65. S. Christian Leadership Conference v. Sessions, 56 F.3d 1281, 1293 n.23 (11th Cir. 1995) (en banc).

66. Collins v. City of Norfolk, 883 F.2d 1232, 1237 (4th Cir. 1989).

race is relevant to the determination. *Second,* among those courts that have held that any candidate, regardless of race, can be minority-preferred, there has been disagreement as to what evidence should be used to determine minority preference.

    Gingles did not settle whether and to what extent the race of a candidate is relevant to the inquiry into minority preference. Justice Brennan's opinion in *Gingles* expressly stated that "it is the *status* of the candidate as the *chosen representative of a particular racial group,* not the race of the candidate, that is important"[67]—but this section of his opinion did not garner a majority of the Justices' votes. Even with respect to the plurality opinion, all of the evidence that Justice Brennan relied upon in affirming the lower court's finding of vote dilution pertained to elections in which black candidates had competed against white candidates.[68]

    Consistent with *Gingles,* the lower courts have found that the minority-preferred candidate can sometimes be a white candidate. For example, in *Ruiz v. City of Santa Maria,* the Ninth Circuit joined other courts in "rejecting the position that the 'minority's preferred candidate' must be a member of the racial minority. To hold otherwise would . . . provide judicial approval to 'electoral apartheid.'"[69] But most courts have not adopted Justice Brennan's position that the candidate's race is completely irrelevant, and have found that the race of candidates can be relevant in identifying minority-preferred candidates.[70] Some courts require a lower quantum of evidence to demonstrate that a minority candidate is minority-preferred,[71] while others have held minority and non-minority candidates to the same evidentiary standard.[72]

---

67. Gingles, 478 U.S. 30, 68 (1986) (plurality opinion).

68. *Id.* at 41, 59–60, 80–81 (appendices).

69. Ruiz v. City of Santa Maria, 160 F.3d 543, 551 (9th Cir. 1998) (internal citations omitted).

70. *See, e.g., id.* at 551 ("Most circuits have rejected Justice Brennan's position on the lack of importance of a candidate's race.").

71. For discussion of such cases, *see* Ellen Katz et al., *Documenting Discrimination in Voting: Judicial Findings Under Section 2 of the Voting Rights Act Since 1982,* 39 U. MICH. J. L. REFORM 643, 666 n.111 (2006) (citing Sanchez v. Colorado, 97 F.3d 1303, 1320–21 (10th Cir. 1996); Jenkins v. Red Clay Consol. Sch. Dist. Bd. of Educ., 4 F.3d 1103, 1129 (3d Cir. 1993); De Grandy v. Wetherell, 815 F. Supp. 1550, 1572–73 (N.D. Fla. 1992); Citizens for a Better Gretna v. City of Gretna, 636 F. Supp. 1113, 1133 (E.D. La. 1986), *aff'd,* 834 F.2d 496 (5th Cir. 1987)).

72. *See, e.g.,* Ruiz, 160 F.3d 543, 549–50; Lewis v. Alamance County, 99 F.3d 600, 615 (4th Cir. 1996); Gomez v. City of Watsonville, 863 F.2d 1407,

Courts that have been reluctant to identify white candidates as minority-preferred have expressed uncertainty about whether the white candidate supported by minority voters represents their considered preference, and whether the capacity to elect a candidate of choice, as long as that candidate is white, demonstrates an absence of racial polarization. As one court explained, "when there are only white candidates to choose from[,] it is virtually unavoidable that certain white candidates would be supported by a large percentage . . . of black voters."[73] Some courts thus have held that elections in which only white candidates participate (white-versus-white races) should not be considered at all in determining whether voting patterns exhibit legally significant racial polarization because minority voters cannot be said to have truly equal electoral opportunity if they can elect only their favorite *white* candidates. As one court stated:

> When white bloc voting is 'targeted' against [minority] candidates, [minority] voters are denied an opportunity enjoyed by white voters, namely the opportunity to elect a candidate of their own race. If [minority] voters nevertheless are able to elect many or most of their preferred candidates who are white, a court that refuses to consider candidate race will be unable to conclude that the white majority votes sufficiently as a bloc to enable it . . . *usually* to defeat the minority's preferred candidate. . . . But the Act's guarantee of equal opportunity is not met when, . . . 'candidates favored by [minorities] can win, but only if the candidates are white.'"[74]

Most courts have opted for a middle ground, refusing to exclude white-versus-white elections altogether, but giving more weight to elections involving minority candidates.[75] In making these assessments, courts

---

1416 (9th Cir. 1988); Black Political Task Force v. Galvin, 300 F. Supp. 2d 291, 303 (D. Mass. 2004), *aff'd*, 543 U.S. 997 (2004); Rodriguez v. Pataki, 308 F. Supp. 2d 346, 388–89 (S.D.N.Y. 2004); Armour v. Ohio, 775 F. Supp. 1044, 1057 (N.D. Ohio 1991).

73. Westwego Citizens for a Better Gov't v. City of Westwego, 872 F.2d 1201, 1208 n.7 (5th Cir. 1989) (internal quotation marks omitted; ellipsis in original); *see also* Lewis v. Alamance County, 99 F.3d 600, 605 (4th Cir. 1996).

74. Ruiz, 160 F.3d 543, 552 (alternations in original; third ellipsis added; citation omitted).

75. Rural W. Tenn., 209 F.3d 835, 840–41; Davis v. Chiles, 139 F.3d 1414, 1417 & n.5 (11th Cir. 1998); Sanchez, 97 F.3d 1303, 1320–21; Uno v. City of

have taken several different approaches. Some courts have looked not only at electoral results but also at additional factors, such as minority financing of candidates, the extent to which candidates campaigned in minority areas, and the reasons minority candidates might not have run in the election.[76] Others have explicitly rejected this approach and use an objective test that considers only which candidate receives the most votes from minority voters.[77] In practice, many courts do not hold to a strict division between these approaches, relying on elements of both.[78]

Courts have also faced difficulties in deciding how to weigh and assess primary elections and multi-candidate elections when identifying the minority-preferred candidate. Some courts have used primary elections as a way of assessing minority-preferred candidates, especially when these elections represent some of the only competitive races in a district, or when there is reason to believe minority support for a candidate in a general election is premised upon party support (see discussion below on causation).[79] Courts that do so often hold that a general-election candidate supported by a minority group is not necessarily the minority group's choice if another candidate receiving much more support from that minority group failed to advance to the general election.[80] Some courts, however, avoid relying upon party primaries, fearing that the voters who participate in primary elections differ from voters in general election.[81]

Holyoke, 72 F.3d 973, 981, 988 n.8 (1st Cir. 1995); S. Christian Leadership Conf., 56 F.3d 1281, 1303; Clarke v. City of Cincinnati, 40 F.3d 807, 812 (6th Cir. 1994); Nipper v. Smith, 39 F.3d 1494, 1540 (11th Cir. 1994) (en banc); Jenkins v. Red Clay School Dist., 4 F.3d 1103, 1125–29 (3d Cir. 1993); Magnolia Bar Ass'n v. Lee, 994 F.2d 1143, 1149 (5th Cir. 1993). It is not uncommon for a court, despite declaring that white-versus-white elections are potentially relevant, to consider only elections involving minority candidates. *See, e.g.,* Gomez v. City of Watsonville, 863 F.2d 1407 (9th Cir. 1988); City of Carrollton Branch of the NAACP v. Stallings, 829 F.2d 1547 (11th Cir. 1987).

76. *See, e.g.,* Sanchez, 97 F.3d 1303, 1320–21; Jenkins, 4 F.3d 1103, 1129.

77. Ruiz, 160 F.3d 543, 552.

78. Ellen Katz et al., *supra* note 71, at 667 & n.118.

79. *See, e.g.,* Black Political Task Force v. Galvin, 300 F. Supp. 2d 291, 305–06 (D. Mass. 2004).

80. Ruiz, 160 F.3d 543, 551.

81. Katz et al., *supra* note 71, at 670 n.134.

b. Should One Look at Results from "Exogenous" Elections?

Another issue that arises in the context of the polarized-voting inquiry is whether a court should consider election results from races for different offices than those at issue—and, if so, whether the electorate for the two offices can differ without making the evidence irrelevant. For example, in a case involving a state legislative district, should a court consider the vote in a gubernatorial election in the district? Or can it look to the results of the presidential election? The relevance of such "exogenous" elections is especially important where a court considers only campaigns involving white candidates, since there may not have been enough minority candidacies for the office at issue to conduct an adequate statistical analysis of racial bloc voting.

Some courts have refused to consider "exogenous" elections in Section 2 cases.[82] Others have allowed such elections to play only a very minimal role in the court's deliberation.[83] Many courts have allowed evidence from exogenous elections while noting that these elections are less probative of the ability of minority candidates to elect the candidate of their choice.[84] And a few courts have placed a great deal of weight on the exogenous elections.[85]

---

82. *See, e.g.*, City of Carrollton Branch of the NAACP, 829 F.2d 1547, 1560.

83. *See, e.g.*, Smith v. Clinton, 687 F. Supp. 1310, 1317 (E.D. Ark. 1988) ("Nor are we persuaded by evidence of some success by black candidates in school-board elections or other local races, because the electoral structure at issue here has no effect on these candidates.").

84. *See, e.g.*, NAACP v. Fordice, 252 F.3d 361, 370 (5th Cir. 2001) (stating that "Wilson correctly observes that exogenous elections are less probative than elections for the particular office at issue, but he fails to fully address the critical evidentiary reality that 'the exogenous character of . . . elections does not render them nonprobative . . . .'" (quoting Rangel v. Morales, 8 F.3d 242, 247 (5th Cir. 1993) (alteration in original)); *see also* Rural W. Tenn., 209 F.3d 835, 841 (discounting the results of exogenous elections, and instead relying primarily on the results of 10 recent endogenous elections involving both black and white candidates); Clark v. Calhoun County, 88 F.3d 1393, 1397 (5th Cir. 1996) (stating that results of exogenous elections are "less probative" and of "limited relevance")).

85. *See, e.g.*, Meza v. Galvin, 322 F. Supp. 2d 52, 69 (D. Mass. 2004) (finding that evidence of a successful senate and city council run by Hispanic candidates suggested that plaintiffs had failed to sufficiently demonstrate bloc voting on the part of the majority); Garza v. County of Los Angeles, 756

In general, courts have endorsed a "flexible approach to the evidence."[86] These courts have considered the results of exogenous elections where the available data are otherwise sparse or where the exogenous elections involve minority candidates.[87] In *Citizens for a Better Gretna v. City of Gretna*[88] for instance, the Fifth Circuit considered evidence from two statewide races involving black candidates—Jesse Jackson's 1984 bid for the Democratic presidential nomination and a 1979 election for Louisiana's Secretary of State—because the court had statistical data for only two alderman seat elections in which black-preferred candidates had competed.[89] Whether exogenous elections should be considered will likely become a hotly disputed issue during the upcoming redistricting cycle as parties dispute the significance of, and the data regarding, the election of President Obama.

c. How Many Elections Should Be Analyzed?

Another question related to the reliability of the data used in the racially polarized voting inquiry is how many past elections a court should consider. This decision turns on two factors that are at cross-purposes. On the one hand, more electoral results means more data, which in turn means more reliable statistical conclusions. On the other hand, circumstances often change over time, so the information gleaned from old elections may no longer be probative.

In *Gingles*, the Supreme Court stated a clear preference for data spanning some significant period of time. "Because loss of political power through vote dilution is distinct from the mere inability to win a particular election," the Court explained, "a pattern of racial bloc voting that extends over a period of time is more probative . . . than are the results of a single election."[90] In *Gingles* itself, the Court rested its conclusion pri-

---

F. Supp. 1298, 1335–36 (C.D. Cal. 1990) (relying primarily on exogenous rather than endogenous elections, where "relatively marginal" Hispanic candidates had repeatedly failed to gain significant minority support, to make a finding of Hispanic political cohesiveness).

86. Jenkins, 4 F.3d 1103, 1134.

87. Goosby v. Town Bd. of Town of Hempstead, 180 F.3d 476, 497 (2d Cir. 1999); Sanchez, 97 F.3d 1303, 1324–25; Clark v. Calhoun County, 88 F.3d 1393, 1397 (5th Cir. 1996); S. Christian Leadership Conf. v. Sessions, 56 F.3d 1281, 1293 (11th Cir. 1995); Jenkins, 4 F.3d 1103, 1134.

88. 834 F.2d 496 (5th Cir. 1987).

89. *Id.* at 502 & n.15.

90. Gingles, 478 U.S. 30, 57 (citation omitted).

marily on the basis of three election cycles.[91] But, the Supreme Court added, the number of elections that must be studied "will vary according to pertinent circumstances."[92] For instance, "where a minority group has begun to sponsor candidates just recently," only a few elections may be available for examination.[93]

Courts' experiences since *Gingles* have made clear that the number of years examined will vary depending on the circumstances. In *Jenkins v. Red Clay Consolidated School District Board of Education*,[94] the Court of Appeals for the Third Circuit looked as far back as 10 years to analyze several election cycles.[95] In *Gretna*, meanwhile, the Fifth Circuit rested its decision on evidence from only two elections.[96]

How far back a court will go in analyzing election results may ultimately turn on whether a court has "multiple electoral contests" to analyze. If there are multiple *recent* electoral contests (whether "exogenous" or "endogenous") available for analysis, it is less likely that a court will look to the past. Where, however, there are fewer recent elections to examine, a court is more likely to resort to such history.[97]

4. What Constitutes "Legally Significant" Racially Polarized Voting?

As the *Gingles* test makes clear, a successful Section 2 claim entails more than mere racially polarized voting. The racial polarization must be "legally significant." There are at least two questions related to the concept of "legal significance." *First*, can the *reasons* underlying the racial polarization ever be relevant to a vote dilution inquiry? That is, should evidence that racial polarization is due to factors other than race defeat a vote dilution claim? *Second*, what degree of racial-bloc voting must exist for a successful vote dilution claim? At what point is white-bloc voting so great that it will "usually . . . defeat the minority's preferred candidate?"

---

91. *Id.* at 80–81 (appendices).

92. *Id.* at 57 n.25.

93. *Id.* The court also stressed that the *Gingles* test sometimes can be satisfied even if *some* elections were not racially polarized.

94. 4 F.3d 1103 (3d Cir. 1993).

95. *Id.* at 1130.

96. Gretna, 834 F.2d 496, 502–03.

97. *See, e.g.*, Hines v. Mayor and Town Council of Ahoskie, 998 F.2d 1266, 1272 (4th Cir. 1993); Baird v. Consol. City of Indianapolis, 976 F.2d 357, 359 (7th Cir. 1992).

a. Are the Reasons for Racial Polarization Relevant?

On its face, the *Gingles* test does not seem to require that race be the sole cause of racially polarized voting. Nevertheless, judges—including Supreme Court Justices—have reached different conclusions with respect to whether evidence of the reasons for racial polarization is relevant.[98] In a section of *Gingles* that commanded only four Justices' votes, Justice Brennan endorsed the view that the reasons for racial polarization have no bearing on the Section 2 inquiry.[99] However, Justice O'Connor, writing for herself and three other Justices, reached a different conclusion. Justice O'Connor argued that evidence that a minority-preferred candidate was rejected by white voters for reasons other than race "would seem clearly relevant in answering the question whether bloc voting by white voters will consistently defeat minority candidates. Such evidence would suggest that another candidate, equally preferred by the minority group, might be able to attract greater white support in future elections."[100]

Lower courts have taken a number of approaches when considering the role of causation in evaluations of racially polarized voting. At least nine circuit courts of appeals consider the reasons for racial polarization, either implicitly or explicitly.[101] And a number of courts have held that a plaintiff cannot win a Section 2 case where racially polarized voting is caused by reasons other than racial animus.[102] These courts highlight the fact that Section 2 speaks of the denial or abridgement of the right to vote "*on account of race or color*" (emphasis added). In considering causation, most courts do not require plaintiffs to disprove that factors other than race caused divergent voting patterns, but instead require plaintiffs to demonstrate that voting patterns have a causal linkage to race when defendants proffer evidence supporting an alternative explanation.[103]

It can be difficult to demonstrate that race is the underlying cause of racial polarization, especially because minority voting patterns often track

---

98. The Eleventh Circuit has considered the issue twice, only to split evenly on both occasions. *See* Solomon v. Liberty County, 899 F.2d 1012 (11th Cir. 1990) (en banc); Nipper v. Smith, 39 F.3d 1494 (11th Cir. 1994) (en banc).

99. Gingles, 478 U.S. 30, 61–64 (plurality opinion).

100. *Id.* at 100 (O'Connor, J., concurring in the judgment).

101. *See* Ellen Katz et al., *supra* note 71, at 671 n.138 (collecting cases).

102. *E.g.*, Clarke v. City of Cincinnati, 40 F.3d 807, 812–14 (6th Cir. 1994); LULAC v. Clements, 999 F.2d 831, 850–54 (5th Cir. 1993) (en banc).

103. *See* Ellen Katz et al., *supra* note 71, at 671 (discussing cases).

partisan voting. One of the strongest determinants of voting behavior, other than race, is a voter's party identification. Thus, a court may question whether party affiliation, rather than race, explains differences in the voting patterns of white and minority voters. For example, political party affiliation may in part explain minority voters' preferences for a minority Democrat running against a white Republican. And in some areas, race and party affiliation may be so closely correlated that it is difficult to separate the two. One possible way to control for the effect of party identification is to analyze results from party primary elections, as discussed earlier, where presumably all the voters share the same partisan leanings. But the connection between race and party may be too complex to assess merely by examining primary elections.

b.   What Degree of Racial Bloc Voting Is Legally Significant?

The *Gingles* test requires a certain degree of racial bloc voting before it is considered "legally significant." The Court explained that this "legally significant" threshold is intended to distinguish between structural vote dilution and the "mere loss of an occasional election."[104] "[I]n general, a white bloc vote that normally will defeat the combined strength of minority support plus white 'crossover' votes rises to the level of legally significant white bloc voting."[105] The Court in *Gingles*, however, refused to specify the point at which racially polarized voting would become legally significant and stated that there is "no simple doctrinal test for the existence of legally significant racial bloc voting."[106] Rather, the Court explained that legal significance would vary "from district to district" and "according to a variety of factual circumstances."[107]

Unfortunately, the law is not clear on what constitutes legally significant bloc voting.[108] As one court put it, "The level of white bloc voting sufficient to defeat a minority preferred candidate varies accord-

---

104. Gingles, 478 U.S. 30, 51 (1986).

105. *Id.* at 56.

106. *Id.* at 58.

107. *Id.* at 55–56, 58.

108. Yet another issue that courts have grappled with is how the third prong defines the word "usually" in the phrase "usually to defeat the minority's preferred candidate." Contrary to the everyday meaning of the word, some courts have stated that "usually" means "something more than just 51%." Lewis v. Almance County, 99 F.3d 600, 606 n.4 (4th Cir. 1996).

ing to a variety of factual circumstances. Thus, no mathematical formula or simple doctrinal test is available to determine whether plaintiffs satisfied the third factor."[109]

In *Gingles* itself, the Supreme Court affirmed a finding of vote dilution where white support for black candidates ranged between 8 percent and 50 percent in primary elections and between 28 percent and 50 percent in general elections.[110] But in *Bartlett v. Strickland,* although the third *Gingles* prong had been conceded by the parties, the Supreme Court noted that it was "skeptical that the bloc-voting test could be satisfied here, for example, where minority voters in District 18 cannot elect their candidate of choice without support from almost 20 percent of white voters."[111] The Court's statement in *Bartlett* could signal an inclination on the Court's members to tighten the conception of legally significant bloc voting.

D. THE "FOURTH PRONG": PROPORTIONALITY

Since the Supreme Court singled it out as a particularly important factor in *Johnson v. De Grandy,*[112] proportionality has become an increasingly crucial issue in Section 2 cases. As a practical matter, if the number of majority-minority voting districts in a given jurisdiction is at least roughly proportional to the minority's share of the relevant population, it may be difficult for Section 2 plaintiffs to prove a violation. If, on the other hand, all three *Gingles* factors are clearly satisfied and the proportion of districts that are majority-minority is substantially smaller than the minority's share of the population, a state may be found liable.

As with the *Gingles* factors, there are a number of issues that arise in the context of evaluating proportionality that still remain uncertain. Proportionality raises the same concerns about the proper population base discussed earlier. In *De Grandy,* the Court expressly declined to rule on this issue.[113] In *LULAC,* the Court appeared to use CVAP as the appropriate measure: "The relevant proportionality inquiry compares the percentage of total districts that are Latino opportunity districts with the Latino share of the citizen voting-age population."[114] Although

---

109. Bone Shirt v. Hazeltine, 336 F. Supp. 2d 976, 1010 (D.S.D. 2004).
110. 478 U.S. 30, 59.
111. Bartlett v. Strickland, 129 S. Ct. 1231, 1244 (2009).
112. 512 U.S. 997 (1994).
113. Johnson v. De Grandy, 512 U.S. 997, 1017 n.14 (1994).
114. LULAC v. Perry, 548 U.S. 399, 403 (2006).

there are many possibilities, most courts have used VAP or CVAP as a population base.[115]

One important question is whether to measure proportionality regionally or statewide. In *De Grandy*, Hispanics constituted 50 percent of the voting-age population in Dade County and made up "supermajorities" in 50 percent of the State House districts located primarily within the county.[116] In contrast, Hispanics constituted 11.7 percent of the voting-age population of the entire state of Florida, meaning that a proportional share of House districts statewide would have been about 14 out of 120. Yet the only districts controlled by Hispanics in the whole state were the nine in Dade County. Clearly, then, the choice of the appropriate geographic scope for measuring proportionality was potentially significant.

The Supreme Court in *De Grandy* analyzed the proportion of Hispanics in the population in relation to the population in Dade County instead of at the state-wide level, and therefore rejected the plaintiff's Section 2 claim. The Court focused on the fact that, during and before the trial, the plaintiffs had failed to frame their dilution claim in statewide terms; both the parties and the district court had focused almost exclusively on the Dade County area.[117] The Supreme Court's decision therefore did not directly answer the issue of local versus statewide proportionality.

In *LULAC*, unlike in *De Grandy*, the parties did frame their claims in statewide terms. The plaintiffs alleged "injury to African American and Hispanic voters throughout the state" and the district court had considered the issue statewide.[118] The Supreme Court concluded that in such cases, proportionality should be considered statewide. But the Court cautioned that considering proportionality statewide does not mean that a state can satisfy Section 2 simply by showing rough proportionality without regard to where majority-minority districts are located and the manner in which they are drawn. The question of whether a minority's voting power has been diluted still requires an "intensely local appraisal"[119] of challenged districts because "the right to an undiluted vote does not be-

---

115. *See* Barnett v. City of Chicago, 141 F.3d 699, 705 (7th Cir. 1998) (citing cases reaching different conclusions, but holding that CVAP is the "proper benchmark for measuring proportionality").
116. De Grandy, 512 U.S. 997, 1014.
117. *Id.* at 1021–22.
118. *See* LULAC v. Perry, 548 U.S. 399, 436 (quotation marks omitted).
119. *Id.* at 437 (quoting Gingles, 478 U.S. at 79).

long to the 'minority as a group,' but rather to 'its individual members.'"[120] The *LULAC* Court re-emphasized that because the Section 2 right protecting against vote dilution is an individual right, "a State may not trade off the rights of some members of a racial group against the rights of other members of that group."[121]

---

120. *Id.* (quoting Shaw v. Hunt, 517 U.S. 899, 917 (1996)).
121. *Id.*

CHAPTER 5

The Constitutional Limits on Racial Gerrymandering

In 1993, in *Shaw v. Reno*,[1] the Supreme Court created a new constraint on the redistricting process, declaring that the excessive and unjustified use of race in redistricting is prohibited by the Equal Protection Clause of the Fourteenth Amendment. Throughout the 1990s, this doctrine played an important role in litigation over redistricting, resulting in the invalidation of plans in Alabama, Florida, Georgia, Louisiana, New York, North Carolina, South Carolina, Texas, and Virginia. Over the past decade, however, the frequency of *Shaw* claims has declined dramatically and districting plans typically have been upheld against such challenges.[2] These developments are due primarily to the Supreme Court's 2001 decision in *Easley v. Cromartie*,[3] which made it much easier for states to argue that their plans were motivated by *political* rather than *racial* considerations.

---

1. 509 U.S. 630 (1993).

2. *See, e.g.*, Prejean v. Foster, 83 F. App'x. 5 (5th Cir. 2003); Rodriguez v. Pataki, 308 F. Supp. 2d 346 (S.D.N.Y. 2004); Johnson-Lee v. City of Minneapolis, No. 02-1139, 2004 WL 2212044 (D. Minn. Sept. 30, 2004), *aff'd*, 170 Fed. App. 15 (8th Cir. 2006); Cano v. Davis, 211 F. Supp. 2d 1208 (C.D. Cal. 2002); Page v. Bartels, 144 F. Supp. 2d 346 (D.N.J. 2001); Wilkins v. West, 571 S.E.2d 100 (Va. 2002).

3. 532 U.S. 234 (2001).

The Supreme Court has phrased the test for a plaintiff bringing a *Shaw* claim in a number of different ways. In 1995, in *Miller v. Johnson*,[4] the Court struck down a Georgia districting plan on the ground that race had been "the *predominant factor* motivating the legislature's decision to place a significant number of voters within or without a particular district."[5] That conclusion will generally follow, the Court explained, where "the legislature subordinated traditional race-neutral districting principles . . . to racial considerations."[6] The test thus requires a court to determine, and then compare, how much the state legislature considered race and how much it considered "traditional race-neutral districting principles." Only if the former considerations outweighed the latter is the district presumptively unconstitutional under the *Miller v. Johnson* test.

One year later, Justice O'Connor reaffirmed that test, but explained it in slightly different terms: "[S]o long as they do not subordinate traditional districting criteria to the use of race for its own sake or as a proxy, States may intentionally create majority-minority districts, and may otherwise take race into consideration, without coming under strict scrutiny. . . . Only if traditional districting criteria are neglected *and* that neglect is predominantly due to the misuse of race" is the district presumptively unconstitutional.[7]

Most recently, in *Easley v. Cromartie*, the Court reaffirmed that a district may be invalidated pursuant to a *Shaw* claim only if "race *rather than* politics *predominantly* explains" the district's boundaries.[8] The Court also stated: "[T]he party attacking the legislatively drawn boundaries must show at the least that the legislature could have achieved its legitimate political objectives in alternative ways that are comparably consistent with traditional districting principles," and that those alternatives "would have brought about significantly greater racial balance."[9]

A. HOW A COURT DETERMINES THAT RACE WAS A FACTOR IN DISTRICTING

A court's inquiry into whether race predominated in the drawing of district lines is very fact-intensive and will therefore vary from case to case.

---

4. 515 U.S. 900 (1995).
5. *Id.* at 916 (emphasis added).
6. *Id.*
7. Bush v. Vera, 517 U.S. 952, 993 (O'Connor, J., concurring).
8. Easley v. Cromartie, 532 U.S. 234, 243.
9. *Id.* at 258.

As a practical matter, though, courts have relied on certain types of evidence as indicia of racial consideration, including district shape and demographics, statements made by legislators and their staff, and the nature of the data used in the districting process.

1. District Shape and Demographics

District shape is one of the principal categories of evidence upon which courts have relied in determining the role that race played in redistricting. The Supreme Court opinions in this area are replete with descriptions of "finger-like extensions," "serpentine district[s]," "narrow and bizarrely shaped tentacles," "hook-like shape[s]," "spindly legs," and "ruffled feathers," to name just a few. As the Supreme Court explained in *Shaw v. Reno* itself, "reapportionment is one area in which appearances *do* matter."[10]

Despite this focus on shape, the Court has made clear that a regular shape is not constitutionally required. So long as a district is not drawn for impermissible reasons, a district may take any shape, even a bizarre one.[11] A "bizarre" or "irregular" shape, however, in conjunction with certain racial and population-density data, may be "persuasive circumstantial evidence that race for its own sake, and not other districting principles, was the legislature's dominant and controlling rationale in drawing its district lines."[12]

The shape of North Carolina's Twelfth Congressional District, for example, was one of the primary reasons the Supreme Court in *Shaw v. Reno* concluded that race played an improper role in that state's redistricting. The district was approximately 160 miles long and, for much of its length, less than a mile wide. The Court described it as winding in a "snakelike fashion" through different neighborhoods in order to "'gobble[] in enough enclaves of black neighborhoods.'" In one instance it sharpened literally to a point before leapfrogging over another district.[13]

Few of the other districts struck down under *Shaw* have been as irregular as North Carolina's Twelfth, yet shape has played a role in each

---

10. Shaw v. Reno, 509 U.S. 630, 647.

11. Bush v. Vera, 517 U.S. 952, 999 (Kennedy, J., concurring).

12. Miller v. Johnson, 515 U.S. 900, 913. Absent any demographic data, a district's unusual shape could also give rise to an inference of political, rather than racial, motivation. *See* Hunt v. Cromartie, 526 U.S. 541, 547 n.3 (1999).

13. Shaw v. Reno, 509 U.S. 630, 635–36 (quotation marks omitted).

case. Courts found, for example, that the districts at issue in Georgia, Texas, and Virginia included "outlying appendages," "fingers," and "wings" that reached out to "grab" minority populations.[14] The court that struck down the Virginia congressional districting scheme, similarly, characterized the Third District as "unwieldy and distended" "fingers," connected to the hub of the district by means of "lightly populated territory, barren stretches of river, or other dubious connectors such as highway exits which appear to be leading the wrong way," divided counties and even cities, "excis[ing]" black populations along the way.[15]

In contrast, most districts that have survived a *Shaw* attack at the Supreme Court level have been relatively compact. Florida's Senate District 21, for instance, was characterized as "'demonstrably benign and satisfactorily tidy.'"[16] It was located entirely in the Tampa Bay area, had an end-to-end distance no greater than most Florida districts, and did not stand out in shape from a number of other districts.[17] Similarly, the California districting scheme at issue in *DeWitt v. Wilson* entailed "[n]o bizarre boundaries"; indeed, the court-appointed special masters who created the plan expressly rejected a number of proposals to create odd-looking districts.[18] On the other hand, the district upheld in *Easley v. Cromartie* was "the most geographically scattered district in North Carolina."[19] The Court nevertheless declined to strike it down because political considerations such as making the district "safe" for the Democratic Party and protecting incumbents also helped explain its unusual shape.

In the 16 years since the Supreme Court decided *Shaw v. Reno*, a pattern seems to have emerged, although the Court has not yet recognized it expressly. Every district that the Court has invalidated under the *Shaw* doctrine has had two key characteristics. First, the minority group's members have constituted more than 50 percent of the district's popula-

---

14. Miller v. Johnson, 515 U.S. 900, 917; Bush v. Vera, 517 U.S. 952, 965, 973, 979 (plurality opinion); Moon v. Meadows, 952 F. Supp. 1141, 1147 (E.D. Va. 1997) (three-judge court), *summarily aff'd*, 521 U.S. 1113 (1997).

15. Moon v. Meadows, 952 F. Supp. 1141, 1147.

16. Lawyer v. Dep't of Justice, 521 U.S. 567, 575, 580 (1997) (citation omitted).

17. *Id.* at 580–81 & n.8.

18. DeWitt v. Wilson, 856 F. Supp. 1409, 1413–15 (E.D. Cal. 1994) (three-judge court), *summarily aff'd in relevant part,* 515 U.S. 1170 (1995).

19. 532 U.S. 234, 263 (Thomas, J., dissenting).

tion,[20] and, second, the district has been drawn using census *blocks* rather than much larger, organic foundational units, such as election precincts or census tracts.[21] A census *block*, which is generally identical to a city

---

20. *Compare* Shaw v. Hunt, 517 U.S. 899, 905–06 (1996) (invalidating a districting plan whose "overriding purpose" was the creation of a district with an African-American voting majority) (quotation marks omitted); Bush v. Vera, 517 U.S. 952, 972–73 (plurality opinion) (invalidating an "exceptional" majority-minority district whose "shape was essentially dictated by racial considerations"); Miller v. Johnson, 515 U.S. 900, 918 (invalidating a majority-minority district when it was "'undisputed that [the district] is the product of a desire by the General Assembly to create a majority black district'") (citations omitted); Silver v. Diaz, 522 U.S. 801 (1997), *summarily aff'g* 978 F. Supp. 96 (E.D.N.Y. 1997) (three-judge court) (invalidating a majority-minority district); *and* Meadows v. Moon, 521 U.S. 1113 (1997), *summarily aff'g* 952 F. Supp. 1141 (E.D. Va. 1997) (three-judge court) (invalidating a majority-minority district), *with* Lawyer v. Dep't of Justice, 521 U.S. 567, 581 (upholding a district in part because it was not a majority-minority district); Quilter v. Voinovich, 523 U.S. 1043 (1998), *summarily aff'g* 981 F. Supp. 1032 (N.D. Ohio 1997) (three-judge court) (declining to apply strict scrutiny to four districts where minority voters did not constitute a majority); *and* DeWitt v. Wilson, 515 U.S. 1170 (1995), *summarily aff'g* 856 F. Supp. 1409 (E.D. Cal. 1994) (three-judge court) (declining to apply strict scrutiny to California's 52 congressional districts, 17 of which were majority-white districts containing a minority population that exceeded 35%).

21. *Compare* Bush v. Vera, 517 U.S. 952, 961–64, 966–67, 972–76 (plurality opinion) (invalidating three districts drawn on a block-by-block basis, which resulted in boundary lines that "interlock 'like a jigsaw puzzle,'" "correlate almost perfectly with race," and are "unexplainable on grounds other than racial quotas established for those districts") (citations omitted); Shaw v. Hunt, 517 U.S. 899, 902, 905–07 (invalidating a district drawn on a block-by-block basis); Johnson v. Miller, 864 F. Supp. 1354, 1377–78 (S.D. Ga. 1994) (three-judge court) (invalidating a district where the legislature split precincts to include African-American voters in the challenged districts and engaged in a "block by block search for black voters to add to the [district]"), *aff'd*, 515 U.S. 900 (1995); Silver v. Diaz, 522 U.S. 801 (1997), *summarily aff'g* 978 F. Supp. 96, 110–11, 118 (invalidating a district that was at points "one-block long," and "curve[d] and weave[d] among street blocks" to pick up minority voters); Meadows v. Moon, 521 U.S. 1113 (1997), *summarily aff'g* 952 F. Supp. 1141, 1147 (invalidating a district drawn "based upon race at the census block level to divide precincts and apportion large numbers of voters based on race into, and out of, the [challenged district]"), *with* Hunt v. Cromartie, 529 U.S. 1014 (2000) (staying the judgment of a district court that had invalidated a plan drawn using whole, undivided precincts); Hunt v. Cromartie, 526 U.S. 541, 548–51, 554 (1999) (reversing the summary judgment of a district

block, on average contains only a few dozen residents. Because the Census Bureau reports relatively little information at the block level other than the total population and racial composition, and because blocks are more likely to be racially homogeneous than larger areas, some redistricters drawing districts on a block-by-block basis may have been tempted to sift adjoining blocks into separate election districts purely on the basis of racial data. That process can result in districts marred by extremely jagged boundaries. By contrast, a census *tract* is more likely to correspond with a readily identifiable neighborhood, because each tract has a population between 2,500 and 8,000 (on average, a population of 4,000) and its boundaries generally follow permanent, visible geographical features, such as roads, highways, rivers, canals, and railroads. Districts composed largely or entirely of whole, undivided census tracts therefore are less likely to have jagged edges or bizarre shapes. Similarly, election precincts generally contain scores of census blocks and hundreds or thousands of residents, and they are neatly nested within political subdivisions such as towns and counties. Reliance on census tracts and precincts can effectively foreclose the extraordinarily detailed, race-based line-drawing that the Supreme Court condemned in *Shaw v. Reno* and *Bush v. Vera* and helps ensure that district boundaries are neither dramatically irregular nor tightly correlated with race. Thus, the shape and demographics of districts built using whole tracts or whole precincts are less likely to generate constitutional concerns.

2. *Statements by Legislators and Their Staff*

As the Supreme Court made clear in *Miller v. Johnson*, bizarre shape is not a necessary element of a successful *Shaw* claim.[22] A plaintiff may use other evidence to prove that race was the predominant factor in the drawing of district lines. One such alternative category of evidence, on which courts have relied heavily in evaluating the role of race in districting, is direct evidence of legislators' motives. Such evidence can itself take a number of forms.

One form of motive evidence, which was invoked in striking down the North Carolina, Georgia, and Texas plans, is the acknowledgment

---

court that had invalidated a plan drawn using whole, undivided precincts); and DeWitt v. Wilson, 515 U.S. 1170 (1995), *summarily aff'g* 856 F. Supp. 1409, 1413–15 (declining to apply strict scrutiny to districts drawn using whole, undivided census tracts).

22. Miller v. Johnson, 515 U.S. 900, 912–13.

after the fact by participants in the districting process that race was an important consideration. In North Carolina, for example, the principal draftsman of the state plan admitted in his testimony at trial that the creation of majority-minority districts was a "principal reason" for the two districts at issue.[23] Similarly, in Georgia, the Court relied on testimony by the operator of the state's reapportionment computer, and the state's own concessions during the course of litigation, that racial considerations dominated the process.[24] As for Texas, the Court supported its conclusion by pointing to testimony by state officials in a previous trial (in defense to charges of political gerrymandering and minority vote dilution).[25] In a more recent case arising in North Carolina, the same type of evidence bolstered the opposite conclusion: After-the-fact affidavits from the two members of the General Assembly who were most active in redistricting stated that the challenged district was designed not with an impermissible racial motive, but rather to protect incumbents and thereby preserve the existing partisan balance in the state's congressional delegation.[26]

Documents and other evidence produced *during* the districting process are a second form of motive evidence that has been used to support a finding that race was a predominant factor in districting. In concluding that race was used impermissibly in the drawing of Texas's districts, for example, the Court pointed to a letter from a state legislator to the U.S. Department of Justice explaining that race was used as a proxy for political affiliation to protect incumbents.[27] Similarly, the district court that struck down the Virginia districting scheme (in a decision summarily affirmed by the Supreme Court) relied heavily on the state's "General Assembly Guidelines," which prohibited any change to the proposed plan that reduced the percentage of black voters in "the majority black district."[28] On the other hand, the Court upheld a North Carolina district despite contemporaneous comments by a state senator that the state's districting plan "provides for a fair, geographic, racial and partisan balance," and by a legislative staff member that he had "moved Greensboro['s]

---

23. Shaw v. Hunt, 517 U.S. 899, 906.
24. Miller v. Johnson, 515 U.S. 900, 918.
25. Bush v. Vera, 517 U.S. 952, 969-70 (plurality opinion).
26. Hunt v. Cromartie, 526 U.S. 541, 549.
27. Bush v. Vera, 517 U.S. 952, 970 (plurality opinion).
28. Moon v. Meadows, 952 F. Supp. 1141, 1144 (three-judge court), *summarily aff'd*, 521 U.S. 1113 (1997).

Black community into the 12th [district]."[29] The Court concluded that
those statements did not indicate that race had been the predominant
explanation for the district's design.

A third, but related, form of motive evidence, which was used against
Georgia, North Carolina, Texas, and Virginia in striking down their plans,
is a state's submission to the U.S. Department of Justice for preclearance
under Section 5 of the Voting Rights Act. In each of these cases, the
state's preclearance submissions had explicitly acknowledged the racial
motive behind its districting or had made obvious its intent to comply
with the Department of Justice's demands, which the Supreme Court
later characterized as the "maximization" of minority representation.[30]
The district court that invalidated the Virginia plan went so far as to call
it "[s]triking[]" that the state had omitted any reference to race-neutral
criteria in its preclearance submission.[31]

3. The Nature of Reapportionment Data

A third category of evidence that courts have used to evaluate the role
that race played in the redistricting process is the nature of the reapportionment data employed by the state legislature. With the rise of sophisticated computer reapportionment programs in the last few decades, states
are now able to draw districts with very intricately refined boundaries.
Where the data used in this process is particularly sophisticated with
respect to race, it may be used as a basis for a court's finding that race
predominated in the process of drafting the plan.

Such heightened specificity of racial data was an important part of
the cases against both Texas and Virginia. In the Texas case, for instance,
the Supreme Court highlighted the fact that the state's redistricting pro-
gram, "REDAPPL," contained racial data at the block-by-block level,
whereas other data, like party registration and past voting statistics, were
only available at the level of voter tabulation districts (which approxi-
mate election precincts).[32] This fact was used to support the conclusion
that refinements to district boundaries below the level of voter tabulation
districts were due predominantly to race: "Given that the districting software used by the state provided only racial data at the block-by-block
level, the fact that District 30 . . . splits voter tabulation districts and even

29. Easley v. Cromartie, 532 U.S. 234, 253–54 (quotation marks omitted).
30. Miller v. Johnson, 515 U.S. 900, 921–27.
31. Moon v. Meadows, 952 F. Supp. 1141, 1145.
32. Bush v. Vera, 517 U.S. 952, 961–63 (plurality opinion).

individual streets in many places . . . suggests that racial criteria predominated over other districting criteria in determining the district's boundaries."[33] The district court that struck down the Virginia plan reached a similar conclusion.[34] And in *Easley v. Cromartie*, the Court upheld the challenged district in part because the state's redistricting software, unlike the Texas and Virginia programs, *did* provide both racial and political data.[35]

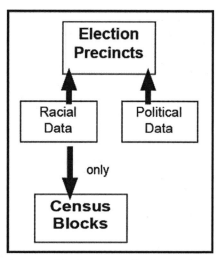

In *Hunt v. Cromartie*, the 1999 decision involving North Carolina's congressional redistricting plan, the Supreme Court relied heavily on an expert affidavit that examined racial data and actual election results for the precincts lying just inside and just outside of the challenged district's border. The expert found a high correlation between the racial composition and the partisan performance of these precincts, suggesting a strong tendency for African-Americans to vote for Democratic candidates. He also found that, where race and party diverged, the district, more often than not, included the more heavily Democratic precinct and excluded the more heavily African-American precinct—which tended to confirm the state's argument that the General Assembly had been motivated more by partisan concerns than by race.[36] The Court reached a similar conclusion in *Easley v. Cromartie*. There, however, the Court downplayed evidence that the state had excluded from the district heavily white precincts with high Demo-

A census block, essentially identical to a city block, permits the Census Bureau to report block level data, such as total population and racial composition. Districts cobbled together from census blocks may raise constitutional concerns.

---

33. *Id.* at 970–71 (plurality opinion).

34. Moon v. Meadows, 952 F. Supp. 1141, 1147 & n.6. See also the discussion above of the relationship between using census blocks (rather than census tracts or election precincts) to draw plans and the resultant districts' shapes and demographics.

35. Easley v. Cromartie, 532 U.S. 234, 249–50.

36. Hunt v. Cromartie, 526 U.S. 541, 549–52.

cratic Party registration on the ground that "registration figures do not accurately predict preference at the polls."[37] The Court was also unpersuaded by evidence that the district could have been made less minority-heavy while equally safe for the Democratic Party through a series of land trades, reasoning that "a showing that the legislature might have 'swapped' a handful of precincts out of a total of 154 precincts, involving a population of a few hundred out of a total population of about half a million, cannot significantly strengthen appellees' case."[38]

Although the *Shaw* doctrine greatly restricts the role of race in redistricting, it does *not* require that states ignore race altogether. The Supreme Court has acknowledged that states will always be *aware* of race when they draw district lines,[39] and has made clear that race may be considered in the process—so long as it does not "subordinate" traditional race-neutral principles and political considerations. Indeed, a current majority of the Court has indicated expressly that a state may intentionally create majority-minority districts under some circumstances.[40] Unfortunately, the precise role that race can play in redistricting under *Shaw* is not totally clear at this time, and may change further in the coming years (particularly if the composition of the Supreme Court changes). For now, however, it appears that race can play *some* role in the process, as one factor alongside traditional race-neutral districting principles and political considerations.

B. TRADITIONAL DISTRICTING PRINCIPLES AND POLITICAL CONSIDERATIONS

It is important, in any event, that a state conform to traditional districting principles to a large degree. Though none of these principles is constitutionally required, they are "objective factors that may serve to defeat a claim that a district has been gerrymandered on racial lines."[41] Similarly,

---

37. Easley v. Cromartie, 532 U.S. 234, 245.
38. *Id.* at 256–57.
39. Shaw v. Reno, 509 U.S. 630, 646 (1993).
40. Bush v. Vera, 517 U.S. 952, 958 (plurality opinion); *id.* at 1008–09 & n.7 (Stevens, J., dissenting); *id.* at 1065 (Souter, J., dissenting). Justices Thomas and Scalia have made clear that they would presume that the intentional creation of majority-minority districts is unconstitutional under any circumstances. *See id.* at 999–1000 (Thomas, J., joined by Scalia, J., concurring in the judgment).
41. Shaw v. Reno, 509 U.S. 630, 647.

evidence that a district was drawn for *political* purposes tends to undercut allegations that its design was motivated primarily by *racial* considerations.

It is not possible to list precisely all "traditional race-neutral districting principles" and valid political considerations since such principles and considerations may vary from state to state. Moreover, the Supreme Court has been hesitant to designate any such list as "comprehensive" given that no one factor is constitutionally required and that redistricting is—within the bounds of federal constitutional and statutory law—a state prerogative. Nevertheless, the existing court opinions pertaining to *Shaw* claims provide some guidance as to the districting principles and political considerations that can assist in defeating a racial gerrymandering charge. Though the list is not exhaustive, there are six such factors in particular: compactness, contiguity, respect for political subdivisions, respect for communities of interest, protection of incumbents, and pursuit of partisan advantage.

1. Compactness[42]

The Supreme Court has repeatedly cited geographical "compactness" as one of the traditional districting principles that can serve to defeat a racial gerrymandering charge.[43] Unfortunately, there is no single measure of compactness that is generally accepted by social scientists as definitive, and the Court has not given a precise definition of the term. Following *Shaw v. Reno*, however, Professors Rick Pildes and Richard Niemi proposed two quantitative measures of compactness for the evaluation of districting plans: a "dispersion" measure, which captures how tightly packed or spread out a district is by calculating the ratio of the district's area to the area of the minimum circle that could circumscribe it; and a "perimeter" measure, which captures the irregularity or jaggedness of the district's border by calculating the ratio of the district's area to the square of the district's perimeter.[44]

---

42. See also the discussion above of compactness in the context of *Gingles*'s first prong.

43. Bush v. Vera, 517 U.S. 952, 962 (plurality opinion); Shaw v. Hunt, 517 U.S. 899, 905–06 (1996); Miller v. Johnson, 515 U.S. 900, 916 (1995); Shaw v. Reno, 509 U.S. 630, 647.

44. Richard H. Pildes & Richard G. Niemi, *Expressive Harms, "Bizarre Districts," and Voting Rights: Evaluating Election-District Appearances After* Shaw v. Reno, 92 MICH. L. REV. 483, 554 & n.200, 555 & n.203 (1993).

The Supreme Court has relied on the results of the Pildes-Niemi study to support its conclusions with respect to the irregularity of districts' shapes,[45] but the Court has not endorsed their approach expressly. Indeed, the Court has not made clear whether one should use a quantitative approach at all, or whether an intuitive, "eyeball" approach is preferable. Nor has the Court made clear how important compactness is in the mix of things: In the Georgia case, the Court focused more on the concentration of minority voters in the outer reaches

	Low perimeter score	High perimeter score
Low dispersion score		
High dispersion score		

Professors Pildes and Niemi proposed two quantitative measures of compactness: the dispersion measure and the perimeter measure. The Supreme Court has relied on the Pildes-Niemi study.

of the Eleventh Congressional District than on the district's shape.[46] Nevertheless, compactness is clearly important: The geometry of North Carolina's Twelfth District was one of the primary reasons the Court gave for its unconstitutionality, even though the state constitution did not require compactness.[47]

2. Contiguity

A second traditional race-neutral districting principle that can help defeat a *Shaw* claim is "contiguity."[48] A district may be defined as contiguous if one can reach any part of the district from any other part without crossing the district boundary—in other words, if the district is not divided into two or more discrete pieces. (An intervening body of water, such as in Florida's Senate District 21, does not necessarily undermine a district's contiguity.)[49] Contiguity has been described as a "relatively trivial

---

45. *See, e.g.*, Bush v. Vera, 517 U.S. 952, 960, 973 (plurality opinion).
46. Miller v. Johnson, 515 U.S. 900, 917.
47. Shaw v. Hunt, 517 U.S. 899, 934–35 (Stevens, J., dissenting).
48. Lawyer v. Dep't of Justice, 521 U.S. 567, 581 n.9; Miller v. Johnson, 515 U.S. 900, 916; Shaw v. Reno, 509 U.S. 630, 647.
49. Lawyer v. Dep't of Justice, 521 U.S. 567, 581 & n.9.

requirement and usually a noncontroversial one,"[50] and indeed there are very few districts that are even arguably noncontiguous. Nevertheless, the fact that North Carolina's Twelfth District was only "point contiguous"—*i.e.*, that in one instance it remained connected at only a single point, like the red squares on a checkerboard—certainly contributed to the Court's conclusion that it was unconstitutional.[51]

3. Respect for Political Subdivisions

A third traditional districting principle cited by the Supreme Court is "respect for political subdivisions."[52] Redistricting plans exhibit "respect" for political subdivisions by creating districts that do not needlessly cross county or municipal boundaries—in other words, by keeping counties, cities, and towns intact, where possible. Lack of such respect can cause "severe disruption of traditional forms of political activity."[53]

A district is defined as contiguous if one can reach any part of the district from any other part of the district without crossing a district boundary.

A lack of respect for political subdivisions was one of the major reasons for the invalidation of the Georgia, North Carolina, Texas, and Virginia plans. Georgia's Eleventh District encompassed portions of three urbanized counties, one of which was split among four congressional districts,[54] while in North Carolina, the Twelfth District split ten counties and six cities.[55] In Virginia, the invalidated Third Dis-

50. Bernard Grofman, *Criteria for Districting: A Social Science Perspective*, 33 UCLA L. Rev. 77, 84 (1985).

51. Shaw v. Reno, 509 U.S. 630, 636.

52. *Id.* at 647; Miller v. Johnson, 515 U.S. 900, 916.

53. Bush v. Vera, 517 U.S. 952, 974 (plurality opinion).

54. Miller v. Johnson, 515 U.S. 900, 908.

55. Shaw v. Reno, 509 U.S. 630, 636.

trict divided 11 of the 17 localities that it touched.[56] And in Texas, the invalidated plan exhibited "utter disregard of city limits."[57]

On the other hand, a lack of respect for political subdivisions will not necessarily lead to the invalidation of a plan, as the Supreme Court made clear in *Lawyer v. Department of Justice*.[58] The legislative district at issue in that case, Florida's Senate District 21, split three counties, yet it nevertheless met with Supreme Court approval. The Court explained that split counties are a "common characteristic[]" of Florida legislative districts, due to "the State's geography and the fact that 40 Senate districts are superimposed on 67 counties."[59] One should not assume, however, that exhibiting respect for political subdivisions will necessarily immunize a districting plan from attack. In *Abrams v. Johnson*,[60] the Supreme Court objected to a proposed Georgia plan even though the districts followed county lines almost perfectly.[61]

4. Respect for Communities of Interest

A fourth traditional districting principle consistently enumerated by the Supreme Court is "respect for . . . communities defined by actual shared interests."[62] Indeed, the Court has made clear that a state may recognize communities that have a particular racial makeup, "provided its action is directed toward some common thread of relevant interests."[63] But this common thread must be "tangible"—a "mere recitation of purported communities of interest" is insufficient.[64] More important, such a common thread must extend beyond race itself. In *Miller v. Johnson*, for example, the Court rejected the argument that Georgia's majority-minority Eleventh District encompassed a community of interest in combining the "black neighborhoods of metropolitan Atlanta and the poor black populace of

56. Moon v. Meadows, 952 F. Supp. 1141, 1147 (E.D. Va. 1997) (three-judge court), *summarily aff'd*, 521 U.S. 1113 (1997).

57. Bush v. Vera, 517 U.S. 952, 974 (plurality opinion).

58. 521 U.S. 567 (1997).

59. *Id.* at 581.

60. 521 U.S. 74 (1997).

61. The proposed plan did, however, split one county in the Atlanta metropolitan area, as well as one non-metropolitan county that had "never before [been] split in apportionment plans." *Id.* at 89.

62. Miller v. Johnson, 515 U.S. 900, 916.

63. *Id.* at 920.

64. *Id.* at 919.

coastal Chatham County."[65] The two regions, the Court declared, were "260 miles apart in distance and worlds apart in culture": The "social, political and economic makeup of the Eleventh District [told] a tale of disparity, not community."[66] In contrast, the Court accepted a community-of-interest justification in *Lawyer v. Department of Justice*, since the predominantly urban, low-income residents of Florida's Senate District 21 "'regard themselves as a community.'"[67] Moreover, "[e]vidence indicated that District 21 [is] the poorest of the nine districts in the Tampa Bay region and among the poorest districts in the State, whose white and black members alike share a similarly depressed economic condition . . . and interests that reflect it."[68]

Where a state seeks to defend a district against a *Shaw* attack on the basis of a community of interest, it is important that the state not only show a community's common thread beyond race, but also show that it was aware of such a community *at the time* the plan was framed. Indeed, the Court rejected the community-of-interest justification offered by Texas in *Bush v. Vera* at least in part because the evidence of commonality had not been "available to the Legislature in any organized fashion before [the districting plan] was created."[69]

5. Protection of Incumbents

The Supreme Court also has recognized incumbency protection—at least in the limited form of avoiding contests between incumbents—as a legitimate state goal.[70] Consequently, if a district's lines are due predominantly to incumbency protection, and not to race, a state may be able to

---

65. *Id.* at 908.
66. *Id.*
67. Lawyer v. Dep't of Justice, 521 U.S. 567, 581 (citation omitted).
68. *Id.*
69. Bush v. Vera, 517 U.S. 952, 966 (plurality opinion; quotation marks omitted); *see also* Kelley v. Bennett, 96 F. Supp. 2d 1301 (M.D. Ala. 2000) (three-judge court) (highlighting the lack of evidence that the plan's drafter "knew or cared about these communities of interest when he drew the district lines"), *vacated by* 531 U.S. 28 (2008).
70. Bush v. Vera, 517 U.S. 952, 964–65 (plurality opinion); Easley v. Cromartie, 532 U.S. 234, 248.

defeat an otherwise valid *Shaw* claim.[71] As the Court reasoned in *Easley v. Cromartie*, it was permissible for the legislature to reject an alternative districting plan that "would have pitted two incumbents against each other." The legislature "drew its plan to protect incumbents—a legitimate political goal."[72]

6. Pursuit of Partisan Advantage

Analogously, the Supreme Court has stated that districts may take on unusual shapes and disregard traditional districting principles if they do so in an effort to secure partisan advantage. In *Bush v. Vera*, a plurality of the Justices recognized "otherwise constitutional political gerrymandering" as a legitimate goal that states could pursue through a variety of means that might be suspect in other contexts.[73] According to the Court, "[i]f district lines merely correlate with race because they are drawn on the basis of political affiliation, which correlates with race, there is no racial classification to justify."[74] In *Easley v. Cromartie*, similarly, the Court endorsed the inclusion of heavily African-American precincts in the district at issue where the legislature aimed "to secure a safe Democratic seat" and "sought precincts that were reliably Democratic . . . for obvious political reasons."[75]

7. State-Specific Principles and Other Race-Neutral Redistricting Principles

It is not yet possible to enumerate all traditional race-neutral districting principles that might potentially assist in defeating a claim of unconstitutional racial gerrymandering because such principles will vary from state to state. Indeed, some of the most recent Supreme Court cases have emphasized the jurisdiction-specific nature of the inquiry. In *Lawyer v. Department of Justice*, for instance, the Court considered a number of additional districting principles particular to Florida, including

---

71. *See, e.g.*, Theriot v. Parish of Jefferson, 185 F.3d 477, 485 (5th Cir. 1999) (rejecting a *Shaw* challenge to a majority-black councilperson district, and holding that racial considerations had been "plainly subordinate to the majority of the councilpersons' preoccupation with protecting incumbency and maintaining other political advantages").
72. Easley v. Cromartie, 532 U.S. 234, 248.
73. Bush v. Vera, 517 U.S. 952, 968 (plurality opinion).
74. *Id.*
75. Easley v. Cromartie, 532 U.S. 234, 245, 247.

multicounty districting (to increase the number of legislators who are available to speak for each county) and the desire to avoid out-of-cycle elections.[76] The Court appeared to *de*-emphasize such principles as respect for political subdivisions that were not common to Florida districting. Similarly, in *Abrams v. Johnson,* the Supreme Court approved a court-drawn plan that had considered "Georgia's traditional redistricting principles."[77] These principles were based on maintaining, among other things, district cores, four traditional "corner districts" in the corners of the state, and an urban majority-black district in the Atlanta area.[78]

In sum, race may still be a factor in a state's redistricting process, and at times it must be considered to avoid violating the Voting Rights Act. Commitment to traditional districting principles and responsiveness to political considerations may shield a plan from a constitutional challenge even if race was considered. Under the current state of the law, however, it is not sufficient for a district merely to exhibit *some* respect for traditional districting principles and political concerns—such a district will not be immune from attack if race nonetheless predominated in the process. If a court finds that "[r]ace was the criterion that, in the state's view, could not be compromised," a district may be struck down regardless of its consideration of other factors.[79]

C. OTHER WAYS TO JUSTIFY THE USE OF RACE IN DISTRICTING

If race predominated over traditional race-neutral districting principles and political factors, the district is *presumptively* unconstitutional. But it may be possible, under certain limited circumstances, to overcome that presumption. Indeed, a majority of the justices on the Supreme Court have indicated that an effort to comply with Section 2 or Section 5 of the

---

76. Lawyer v. Dep't of Justice, 521 U.S. 567, 581–82 nn.9–10. Because Florida has staggered senate terms and only half the districts choose a state senator in any given election cycle, the mid-decade redistricting could have resulted in special "out-of-cycle" elections in districts that were significantly redrawn.

77. 521 U.S. 74, 84 (1997).

78. *Id.* The Court's inclusion of this last "principle," the maintenance of a majority-black district, implies that a state may purposefully *maintain* a district for race-related reasons without running afoul of *Shaw*.

79. Shaw v. Hunt, 517 U.S. 899, 907.

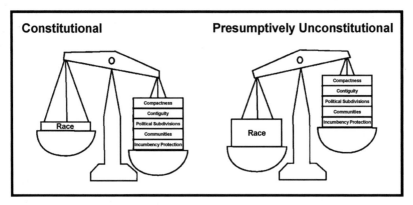

The Shaw *doctrine restricts the use of race in redistricting. Race may only be considered alongside traditional race-neutral factors.*

Voting Rights Act or an effort to remedy past discrimination might justify an otherwise unconstitutional plan.[80]

With regard to Section 2, the state must have had a "strong basis in evidence" *at the time it drew the district* for concluding that the creation of a majority-minority district was reasonably necessary in order to comply with Section 2. "[G]eneralized assumptions about the prevalence of racial bloc voting" would not qualify as a "strong basis in evidence."[81] Moreover, the district must "substantially address[]" the potential Section 2 liability[82] without "subordinat[ing] traditional districting principles to race substantially more than [is] 'reasonably necessary' to avoid" that liability.[83] A district will be held unconstitutional if it is bizarrely shaped and noncompact, it otherwise neglects traditional districting principles,

---

80. Shaw v. Reno, 509 U.S. 630, 653–57 (1993); Miller v. Johnson, 515 U.S. 900, 920–21 (1995); Shaw v. Hunt, 517 U.S. 899, 908–16; Bush v. Vera, 517 U.S. at 976–77 (plurality opinion); *id.* at 990–92 (O'Connor, J., concurring); *id.* at 1033 (Stevens, J., dissenting); *id.* at 1065 (Souter, J., dissenting).

81. Bush v. Vera, 517 U.S. at 994 (O'Connor, J., concurring).

82. Shaw v. Hunt, 517 U.S. 899, 915, 918.

83. Bush v. Vera, 517 U.S. 952, 979 (plurality opinion); *see also* King v. Ill. Bd. of Elections, 979 F. Supp. 619, 627 (N.D. Ill. 1997) (three-judge court) (holding that Illinois' majority-Hispanic Fourth Congressional District was narrowly tailored to serve the compelling state interest in complying with Section 2 of the Voting Rights Act because the district's "noncompactness and irregularity" could be explained by the desire to maintain the core of a neighboring majority-black district that separated Chicago's two densely populated Hispanic enclaves), *summarily aff'd,* 522 U.S. 1087 (1998) (summarily affirming the district court's judgment, over the objections of Justices Scalia, Kennedy, and Thomas).

and it deviates substantially from a hypothetical court-drawn Section 2 district *for predominantly racial reasons.*[84]

Similarly, it is not entirely clear when a presumptively unconstitutional district can be saved by the argument that it was drawn to comply with Section 5 of the Act. In *Bush v. Vera,* the state of Texas made that argument in defense of District 18 in Houston, but a five-justice majority rejected it. Under the benchmark plan that was in effect prior to the 1991 redistricting, District 18's population was only 35.1 percent African-American. Under the 1991 plan, that figure rose to 50.9 percent. Because the state had not demonstrated that this increase in black population "was necessary to ensure nonretrogression" under Section 5, the Court struck down District 18.[85] The Court did not explain when, if ever, an increase in a district's minority population would be "necessary to ensure nonretrogression." Nor did the Court even begin to address the thornier questions, such as when and how changes in levels of "crossover" voting would affect a state's ability to use compliance with Section 5 as a defense to a *Shaw* claim.

With regard to past discrimination, the legislature must likewise have a "strong basis in evidence" that remedial action is necessary *before* engaging in it, and must identify "with some specificity" the discrimination to be remedied.[86]

The Court has never expressly upheld a plan on any of these bases, and in general the Court has been extraordinarily reluctant to hold that *any* racial classification is justified. Furthermore, several Justices have indicated that attempted compliance with the Voting Rights Act should *never* be allowed to justify a racial gerrymander. At this time, therefore, a state may find it too risky to use race as the predominant factor in its districting.

---

84. Bush v. Vera, 517 U.S. 952, 977 (plurality opinion); *id.* at 994 (O'Connor, J., concurring).

85. *Id.* at 983 (plurality opinion).

86. Shaw v. Hunt, 517 U.S. 899, 909–10 (quotation marks omitted); Bush v. Vera, 517 U.S. 952, 982 (plurality opinion).

Index